GW00789327

DEVON EPITAPHS

DEVON EPITAPHS

MICHAEL WELLER

ryelands

First published in Great Britain in 2010

British Library Cataloguing-in-Publication Data
A CIP record for this title is available from the British Library

ISBN 978 1 906551 26 1

RYELANDS
Halsgrove House,
Ryelands Industrial Estate,
Bagley Road, Wellington, Somerset TA21 9PZ
Tel: 01823 653777 Fax: 01823 216796
email: sales@halsgrove.com

Part of the Halsgrove group of companies
Information on all Halsgrove titles is available at: www.halsgrove.com

Printed and bound by SRP Ltd., Exeter

CONTENTS

HOW THIS BOOK CAME TO BE WRITTEN

During the autumn of 2004 I spent a few days teaching in a school on the outskirts of Plymouth. On one particular and especially golden autumn day, having no special wish to engage with colleagues in the staff room over lunch I drove the couple of miles or so to Tamerton Foliot church with the prime intention of looking inside, having found it locked on a previous visit. Again I was disappointed but such is the nature of fate that an inscription on a gravestone caught my eye and became the catalyst for this collection of epitaphs and sepulchral poetry. Here is what I read:

> *Sweet was the bud the promised bloom. Whilst health to it be given. The Lord of mercy thought it fit that it should bloom in Heaven. Her end was peace, her soul at rest. Her earthly work is done. She calmly to his call obeyed & said O Lord thy will be done.*

The grave was that of a young lady who had died in 1867. *At the time* the words struck me as bizarre in the extreme, but worth recording to show to my wife when I arrived home, so I jotted them down on a sheet of paper that was screwed up in my pocket. I think it was the final sentence that seemed so odd at the beginning of the twenty-first century: the idea of acceptance of death as God's will in such a calm manner. Indeed we would nowadays think it unhealthy to think about death even in middle age, such is our expectation of living beyond the *three score and ten years* that scripture allots to us! Indeed female life expectancy in the West Devon area is now a staggering 84.2 years! But before the twentieth century death was an ever present spectre with life expectancy for labourers of only 16 years recorded for the East End of London (Bethnal Green) in the late 1830s! Although in Britain smallpox vaccination came about in the early 1800s, diphtheria, cholera, typhoid and a host of other diseases could carry one off at any time.

I suppose that I should have become aware of epitaphs and graveyard poetry previously, having carried out genealogical research for over thirty years. Although I had often read gravestones and the memorial plaques favoured by the better-off for my own or client's researches I had only concerned myself with dates, places and people, not poetry or prose, which I must confess I had greatly disliked at school! But the fact was that this poem had got me thinking about what other fascinating lines might be out there; after all I was now a teacher and even occasionally actually took poetry lessons! Thus it was not many days before I made my way, notebook in hand to my local churchyard and from there to churches, churchyards and cemeteries further and further afield. My visit to Tamerton Foliot had started me on fascinating quest in which I was to read hundreds of gravestones and memorial tablets. A great many of these were to commemorate people who had *not* reached *three score and ten years*, although many over 60s are included. I have made what I hope is an interesting and I trust a representative selection of around one hundred epitaphs taken from the headstones of the ordinary through the plaques of the professional classes to the monuments of the rich.

NOTE ON THE SCOPE AND DATA OF THE BOOK

Although the intention of the collection was to give a picture of the varying sorts of poetry, verse or other lines that were inscribed on gravestones and other memorials, it quickly became apparent that the inclusion of epitaphs that were not at all poetic but seemed of artistic merit (or of interest by virtue of the sentiments expressed thereon or indeed merely by their use of hyperbole!) would help to further clarify the picture of how our ancestors liked to eulogise the departed and would widen the appeal of the work.

Whilst it might have been tempting to branch out and widen the scope of the work to include comments on the types of material used for gravestones and memorials, and to speculate on the relative merits of granite against marble, alabaster or sandstone and so on, I have avoided it. Similarly I have almost entirely avoided remarks about the style, size, decoration including carvings or reliefs which adorn such monuments especially those found inside churches. These aspects of sepulchral fashion have their own history and merit study in their own right. Thus this book is what it claims to be: a collection of the verse, poetry and eulogy in the English tongue. The main deviation from this course is the inclusion of some genealogical data both where it was obvious that more than one member of a family was buried or commemorated nearby and where its inclusion serves to set the scene, so to speak. The names and dates of death are always included (unless these were unclear or in one or two examples which are relatively recent and might give distress to the living, when I have felt it inappropriate to identify the exact location) as I feel that aspects of the research might be of more than passing interest to the family historian. Ages are also included as the age of the departed, often all too young, is a factor in understanding the choice of words.

Latin epitaphs (of which Devon's churches have a great many) were from the first considered outside the scope of this work because of the relatively few people who can read the language nowadays. I can however recommend John Parker's book *Reading Latin Epitaphs* for those who want to take the subject further.

Most of the research was carried out over a five year period commencing November 2004. To be included I must have personally seen the original and have transcribed it myself; the few exceptions to this are clearly indicated. The epitaphs included are basically a personal choice. The choice has been made largely from churches that I happened to be near with notebook and pencil but also from churches that I travelled specifically to see, the latter case particularly true of those churches often in towns which have provided many of the poems and eulogies favoured by the middle and upper classes. I have, as I believe is correct, defined an epitaph as 'a short piece of writing or a poem about a dead person, especially one written on their gravestone…', although the assumption is also made that a poem chosen to fit, so to speak, the character of the deceased even though it was written for general use, is also an epitaph on the grounds that it says about the deceased what the bereaved, often those from less academic households, would have *wanted* to write had they been sufficiently able.

I have chosen the texts that I personally found fascinating. This may have been because of sheer pathos, or because verses amused me, especially the hyperbole, also because in very few examples they tell a story about the departed. In just a few cases I chose them because the sentiments expressed seemed almost alien to the twentieth-first century mind, and often because *I just liked them*. I have also admired the unquestioning religious beliefs which will have comforted those relatives who paid for the stone. I have tried to include a balanced selection. As a rule of thumb the reader will note that for the most part poetry is found on tombstones in graveyards and cemeteries, eulogies, poems and prose can be found on the plaques and monuments that decorate the inside walls of churches; this is a fact of history and a matter of taste, money and without doubt, of fashion for those who erected the monuments.

By the 1950s Victorian poetry was distinctly out of fashion rather like the Victorian fireplaces that people gladly ripped out of their front rooms and bedrooms (only for their descendants to replace them with reproduction ones 40 or 50 years later). Religious belief has been greatly eroded both by two World Wars and the growth of materialism. The concept of Heaven in terms of a paradise in the sky, a belief often implied by the epitaphs that I have found, as it is also in eighteenth and nineteenth century hymns has undergone some modification even within the Church. The popularity of cremation over the last half century or so has largely obviated the need for tombstones and therefore anything to write on them. Thus they are largely superseded by the 'Book of Remembrance' which for the most part can only contain a few brief words. We simply put *In God's garden* against my father's name. Unlike the fireplaces, I do not think that epitaphs will make a big come-back. However they are still alive and well on the In Memoriam columns of certain local newspapers both in Britain and North America.

This book includes examples which for the most part cover a period from the early seventeenth century until the early twentieth century. By far the greatest coverage is of the Georgian and Victorian periods. Poetry on gravestones remained popular into Edwardian times but was already in decline by 1914. Few examples exist from more recent times – the bereaved, partly under clerical influence preferring less flamboyant or flowery simple sentiments such as: 'Till we Meet', 'In God's Keeping' and short biblical texts. Elaborate marble mural plaques had long been out of fashion, less expensive brass wall plaques expressing more fact and less hyperbole beginning to appear in the third quarter of the nineteenth century.

I hope you enjoy my selection.

WHO WROTE THE EPITAPHS?

It will be apparent from my opening remarks that when I started this collection I had little or no subject knowledge; indeed I do not think that it had ever occurred to me to consider the provenance of the lines that I was reading, with the obvious exception of the ubiquitous quotations from scripture. Indeed, if I had been pushed, I would probably have assumed that the average verses or short eulogies were written by some lettered relative or friend of the deceased.

My searches at first included only gravestones (I was only to include plaques and monuments at a later stage). However I had not been collecting for very long before I started to come across the use of the same lines on more than one headstone, not perhaps in the same churchyard but a few miles distant. At first I assumed that the reason for the common source was a local undertaker who kept a few sets of apt verses in a drawer in case distressed relatives could not provide their own, but that these were nevertheless a purely local source. As I was later to discover this was not entirely removed from the truth. Perplexed, I soon resolved to feed the opening lines of a couple of poems that I had found in Devon churchyards into the *Google* search engine merely to see what would turn up. Whilst by no means did I find every poem that I tried, I had sufficient success to realise the geographical spread of examples of the same poem occurring made it obvious that there must be one or more common sources of these poetic epitaphs. Indeed I was finding them quoted in local history society transcriptions of graveyard inscriptions chiefly in the United States (especially New England) but also in India, Malaya, and Canada; basically in the former colonies as well elsewhere here in Britain. Obvious deduction – there must have been printed books of appropriate texts. Equally apparent therefore was the fact that undertakers all over the English speaking world were using one or more printed set of texts. I tried 'Googling' expressions such as 'books of epitaphs' and other increasingly banal phrases but I couldn't seem to ask the right question.

I even enquired of a history professor at Exeter University but he could not help me either. As luck would have it I found myself at a reception following a lecture at Exeter Cathedral talking to none other than a monumental mason, who soon told me that he did possess such a book of Victorian date which he had rescued from his employers in a clear-out. A few days later the obliging gentleman actually sent me the 1832 volume entitled *The Churchyard Lyrist* containing *Five Hundred Original Inscriptions to Commemorate the Dead* .

The book proved what was now becoming obvious, that both poems, epitaphs and eulogies could be had ready made and copyright free! The writer and editor one G. Mogridge, makes it clear in his foreword that although much is his own composition, he has also collected the contents from other sources; presumably churchyards and churches! In justifying the need for such a publication he notes that : *'....he who is softened and impressed by reflections on the dead is not likely to indulge in bitterness and injustice towards the living.'*

Perhaps a little abashed (because it seems that in being somewhat tardy in publishing Mogridge may have been 'pipped at the post') he states that *'A recent publication has in a degree, supplied the want of original epitaphs, but not so amply as to render the present work unnecessary. The whole of the inscriptions now offered to the public were written sometime before the publication of Doctor Booker made its appearance.'*

So Mogridge was not the first to compile such a volume! Back to Google where I soon discovered that the Reverend Luke Booker had published his *Tributes to the Dead* in 1830, containing over 200 epitaphs many of which were *his* own work, but he also had quarried from other sources.

Even Booker was not the first to publish. Thomas Caldwell's *A Collection of Epitaphs* appeared in 1802, although these and similar works were more antiquarian collections intended for interest rather than for the use of the bereaved. This is not say that some parts of these works too may not have been plagiarised

Two or three of Mogridge's epitaphs are worth quoting here, so that before reading my own collection the reader may see the kind of writing which whilst it might purport to describe one particular unique individual was in fact actually more widely used. In the case of the poetic texts I have found that these are sometimes the subject of a 'pick 'n mix' usage, where lines from two or perhaps three other poems have been mixed to provide what the eulogist wished to say. Where such a poem appears in the collection I have indicated accordingly in the notes.

Suitable for a minister of religion, Mogridge suggests;

> *He will long be remembered as a bright example of piety, and as a possessor of those gifts and graces which eminently adorn a Christian Minister.*

For more general use he includes:

> *The Grave can neither withhold the righteous from happiness nor protect the wicked from unutterable woe.*

The theme of warning and the need to be prepared for death was a common sentiment throughout the nineteenth century.

On a less judgemental note Mogridge recommends for 'Pious Characters':

> *Many Christians like her have lived a life of hope: but few like her have died a death of exultation.*

It is remarkable to note (and some of my own examples of this are included in this anthology) how often the departed are credited with dying well!

Mogridge intended his book as a copyright free resource or quarry for those who were not sufficiently lettered or able to commission their own poet or writer of prose. There were other kinds of collection becoming available; some intended more as an antiquarian collection such as that published in 1857 by Silvester Tissington. Entitled *A Collection of Epitaphs and Monumental Inscriptions on the Most Illustrious Persons of All Ages and Countries* Tissington's book included epitaphs in translation from the Ancient World as well as those likely to be found in the English churchyard or church. It stands to reason however that many readers of this work would have used extracts from this book as well where the verse seemed to fit what *they* wanted to say.

A great critic of the so-called doggerel which appeared on the gravestone was Augustus Hare. In the preface of the first edition of his *Epitaphs for Country Churchyards* published in 1851 he comments '…how almost ludicrous, many of them are.' Hare's contempt especially singles out '…that miserable doggrel (sic) which tells of -

Afflication sore long time I bore,
Physicians were in vain,
Till death gave ease, as God was please,
To ease me of my pain.'

He continues: *'This is only one of many Epitaphs of the same kind…and are often repeated over and over again in the same churchyard. In many places the poor are in the habit of bringing a book, which contains a collection of these churchyard rhymes, to the rector…in order that he may assist them in choosing one…the clergyman has the power of trying to persuade the people to be content with a text of Scripture, or even the name of their friend and the date of his death, instead of the rhyme; but in spite of this we see our churchyards rapidly filled with absurd and almost pagan trash.'*

Hare continued: *'The poor do not need long Epitaphs - they do not care for any depth of meaning or poetry of expression; the more simple the words and thoughts, the more suited to their minds, and the more does the Epitaph come home to their hearts.'*

Thus Hare included in the first section of his book a selection of short texts taken from Holy Scripture, the second section contained brief sentences and the third and final section comprised verses of poetry chiefly from well-known writers

Clearly not all epitaphs are borrowed from Mogridge's, Hare's or indeed anyone else's book. A great many *are* unique. In reading my collection it will be obvious in some cases that this is so and is especially true of the eulogies, although not absolutely so when one recalls Mogridge's epitaph for a clergyman.

During the second year of my research when I had expanded my study to include memorial plaques and monuments inside churches it became readily apparent that most of the verses that I was now transcribing had *not* come from books of epitaphs nor from well known passages of scripture. These were entirely another genre. The educated classes frequently possessed some member of the family with sufficient wit to compose poetry or to write, sometimes with the considerable use of hyperbole, both poems and eulogies; thus many middle and upper class epitaphs are genuinely unique; many of these are included in my collection. Occasionally these classes quoted from classical works or borrowed from other sources which they thought apt. Where possible in the text I have tried to identify or at least speculate on the possible origins of this group of epitaphs.

ARE THE DEPARTED ACTUALLY THERE?

It is also worth noting, that in the case of memorials, ledger stones, plaques etc, normally found inside churches these often only commemorate the departed. They may rest somewhere under the church floor nearby, possibly in a small brick-lined vault; or in the case of a great family in a genuine family size vault accommodating many coffins. It may seem disappointing but vaults are never of the capacious dimensions depicted in horror films of the 1950s and 1960s and the means of entrance to them is rarely if ever clearly advertised. It is also entirely possible that the departed are buried in another parish altogether, possibly depending on where they were living (or staying) at the time of death; or they may actually be in the churchyard. As a rule of thumb one can always assume that those mentioned on a headstone in the churchyard are actually there unless the text says 'In memory of…', in which case one should check the burial register. Indeed I recently noticed on a headstone in Paignton churchyard *In memory* of one James Luxon 'WHO WAS DROWNED *On the Banks of Newfoundland*' in January 1852 aged 18 years. Clearly this young man was a fisherman working off the Grand Banks but his body would not have been repatriated. If the facts are not clearly indicated on the relevant memorial genealogists may wish to consult the parish burial register in the appropriate county record office which should clarify the matter, for if the deceased is not mentioned on the appropriate dates their remains are elsewhere.

DYING YOUNG

The reader will probably be struck and indeed saddened by the relatively large number of children whose epitaphs are included in this publication and indeed also of those who died far too early in their adult life. I think that it is probably a little more likely that those who died young were commemorated with a tangible memorial simply because of the unexpected gap that their premature death left in the hearts of parents and relatives. That is not to say that people prior to the twentieth century expected all their children to live for *three score and ten* years any more they expected to do themselves; death throughout the period was an ever present spectre. Some people did live to a ripe old age but as a percentage of the population this was not a high figure. The first year of life was especially precarious. Figures for 1851 show that in the Bristol area infant mortality was 172 per thousand of live births. The overall figure for England and Wales was 154/1000 for the same period with black spots such as Manchester recording 196/1000. Some improvement took place by the turn of the twentieth century and the overall figure for 2001 was a mere 6/1000. The chief causes of infant mortality were gastro-enteritis, atrophy, tuberculosis, dysentery, diarrhoea, scarlet fever, measles and smallpox. The first year of life, as some of the examples[1] in this book will show, was ever a worry.

In an age before proper ante- and post-natal care and long prior to contraception, a woman's lot in marriage with its multiple pregnancies and resulting childbirth was a risky one. It is easy to speculate that a considerable proportion of women who died below age fifty did so as a result of problems incident on childbirth, haemorrhages chiefly and puerperal fever (a blanket term for all sorts of post-natal infections). Since clotting agents and antibiotics were still far in the future, such deaths were inevitable. Poor antiseptic procedures even amongst doctors did not help matters.

Some women of course sought to avoid the risks of marriage. It has sometimes been speculated that Jane Austen the novelist was one of these, but little good did it do her as she too died before her time (aged 41) in the July of 1817. The cause of her death has been much speculated about, but at the time neither Addison's Disease nor Hodgkin's Lymphoma, which are the two main theories based on her reported symptoms, had been identified. The fact is that prior to 1837 we can only speculate as to exactly why people died except where the cause is stated on headstone or plaque.

Young and old alike were prey to a host of infections and diseases such as smallpox, ever present but often epidemic including a serious outbreak at Okehampton during the summer of 1775. T.B. (then usually known as consumption) was endemic; and there were recurring outbreaks of Cholera which struck much of Devon, notably Exeter and Plymouth in 1831, peaking in 1832. Scarlet fever, measles, diphtheria, typhus, tetanus, sepsis and a host of others could carry off people of any age. However the poor, living in the most cramped and insanitary circumstances especially in the towns and cities were likely to be the worst affected in an epidemic. Nevertheless these infections and diseases were no respecter of class. The Reverend Mr Hughes, the former vicar of Honiton lost his twenty-one year old daughter to consumption at Clannaborough on 26th November 1839.

N.Tryon Still Esq. (at one time a director of the Mount Radford School in Exeter) and his wife Mary eventually settled at Mere in Wiltshire. They suffered much youthful mortality in their offspring as a tablet in the parish church displays. Erected about the year 1836, it runs:

ELEANOR SOPHIA. DIED DEC.21.1805, AGED 3 WEEKS
BURIED AT LOUGHREA CO GALWAY

HENRY TYRON. FEB.1808, 5 MONTHS
BURIED AT HIGHWYCOMBE BUCKS

EMMA, JAN 10.1813, 6 WEEKS
BURIED AT BINGHAM'S MELCOMBE DORSET

GEORGE PARKER, JULY.18.1828, 18 YEARS

ELEANOR SOPHIA, DEC.26:1829, 22
BURIED IN THE SAME GRAVE TO THE SOUTH
OF ST LEONARD'S CHURCH EXETER
SARAH HENRIETTA, MARCH 13:1836, 25 YEARS.

The reader will notice that the couple had more than one child of the same name, after Eleanor's death in 1805, another girl, presumably born in 1806 or 1807 was given her name; this was in no way unusual and probably indicates a desire to perpetuate the name of or to do honour to the memory of another family member. It is not at all unusual to find two living children of the same name especially where a father wished for a son to carry on his name. Thus knowing that a child might well die in infancy two might be named the same in hopes that one would survive to adulthood. However even on a tablet like this which often gives precise genealogical detail the cause of death is rarely mentioned.

The foregoing is not to say that many persons did not live until a reasonable age but the following statistics which are a list of the ages at death from Plymouth (St Budeaux parish) for all those who died between July and the end of December 1814 is not untypical of a growing city:

AGES AT DEATH

4, 76, 5, 0, 0, 0, 77, 26, 0, 61, 2, 65, 68, 63, 37, 23, 82, 33, 6, 0, 65, 64, 25. (0 denotes death of a child *under* one year)

Total number of deaths = 23. Average age at death is exactly 34 years!

At rural East Budleigh at the eastern extremity of Devon where 54 deaths took place in a similar period the average age was almost precisely 43. Furthermore nine of the dead were over eighty years of age and of those three were ninety or over! Only two deaths were of infants under one year. However two decades later (1834) of 26 deaths (July-December) *16* were of children five years or under so matters were by no means consistent.

As previously stated it is not possible to say with precision what the cause of death was in the great majority of cases at least until the introduction of the death certificate in 1837. Parish burial registers (which were required to record the age at death only from 1813) only record the cause of death in the most unusual of cases. A few gravestones or memorials will give this information but often only when a person has died abroad or in the case of an accident. At Cullompton a memorial in the church which records the early deaths of no less than three sons of the Coleman family, notes of Captain Augustus Coleman of the 9th Regiment of Foot, that he had '…died of a Fever in the Island of Grenada…' aged 21 in 1795. His younger brother predeceased him by a few months being '..killed in a Naval Engagement the 14th March 1795 Aged 15.' Horse related accidents were a common cause of death presumably in much the same way as road traffic accidents are today. One could be easily mown down by a horse, the fate of William Baker of Newton St Cyres '…who was killed on the Spot being rode over on the Evening of the 7th Oct. …(1834)' or suffer the unfortunate fate of Ann Pitts '…who was drowned in November last in the Exe, by falling accidentally from a Horse, as she was crossing the River but was not found till the Twenty eight instant …' (which was 28th January 1819). She was buried at Upton Pyne on 30th January. The Upton Pyne register records one further drowning, that of thirteen year old Martha Goff '…who was accidentally drowned at Pynes Mills…' in March 1816 and buried on the 9th of the month. A further example of drowning, this time in the River Yeo near Hayne Bridge is recorded on a plaque in Clannaborough Church near Crediton when both a clergyman's wife and her eighteen year old son were drowned on 29th November 1841 '…IN AN ATTEMPT TO PASS THROUGH THE SWOLLEN WATERS OF THE RIVER…' An even worse fate met Henry Karslake, his wife Sarah and two sons who perished in a fire at their house in South Molton on 30th January 1749. Luckily two children survived the fire including 5 year old Ann who lived to marry twice and die at the good age of 65. This information is found on Ann's memorial plaque in the church, which was erected by her son after her death in 1809.

Life expectancy nowadays is a staggering 77.2 years for males and 81.5 years for women having risen steadily throughout the twentieth century, very significantly so over the last 30 years. Thus we now live within a mind-set which side-lines death as something only to be considered when we are really old – it is not an ever present spectre. Modern life expectancy and infant mortality rates would seem utopian to our Georgian and mid-Victorian ancestors who in the 1840s would on average be lucky to see fifty years and that only for the better off in rural districts.

EPITAPHS FROM GRAVESTONES AND MEMORIALS TO CHILDREN

HONITON (ST MICHAEL – THE FORMER PARISH CHURCH)

On the gravestone of John Pickwick who died on 15th November 1881 aged 12 years, I found this verse…

'TEACH ME TO LIVE THAT I MAY DREAD
THE GRAVE AS LITTLE AS MY BED
TEACH ME TO DIE THAT SO I MAY
RISE GLORIOUS AT THE AWFUL DAY'…

Which comes from Thomas Ken's poem of 1695 and has long been set to music and used as an evening hymn known by the first line which runs: 'All praise to Thee, my God this night.' Still in use today the hymn was sufficiently well-known in the nineteenth century for Thomas Hardy to put it into the mind of his enigmatic character Jude in the novel *Jude the Obscure.*

GULWORTHY (ST PAUL)

Rosina Gulley granddaughter of Robert and Elizabeth Gulley.
Died 16th November 1867 aged 10 years and 8 months.

The following part of this inscription is in italics and the second piece is in Roman script:

Farewell Rosina, Lovely Dear!
Our parting caus'd us many a tear,
The Lord saw fit to call you home,
We must submit, 'His will be done.'

Then follows:

My stay on earth was short,
But glory be to God;
I lay my sins on Jesus,
The atoning Lamb of God.

GULWORTHY (ST PAUL)

This little boy that pass'd so soon
To you bright world above
Has left his friends on earth to mourn
The child they so much loved.

William Voaden son of Thomas and Grace Voaden.
Died 27th June 1864, aged 8 Years.

PANCRASWEEK (ST PANCRAS)

In early life they wisely sought their God,
And bore with rev'rence his chastening rod,
They lov'd the church,
On Christ alone rely'd,
And cheer'd by faith,
In hope and comfort died.

Grave of Mary Susan daughter of Richard and Mary S. Hodge (his late wife). The child having died 28th July 1862 aged 14 years. This grave also holds the mortal remains of Charlotte Hodge who died 13th August the same year (1862) aged 20 years.

At the base of the stone an apt passage from I Samuel 1:23 is quoted '...in their death they were not divided...'

The main text clearly came from an undertaker's book as is proven by this variant from Arnos Vale cemetery, Bristol which displays the 'pick n' mix' method of making up an epitaph:

In early life she wisely sought her god
And with submission bore his chastening rod.
Taught by his spirit she his truth revered
And faith in Christ her dying moments cheered.
Thus blest with grace that heaven alone can give
She learned to die ere thousands learned to live.

BRIDESTOWE (ST BRIDGET)

To us for sixteen anxious months,
His infant smiles were given,
And then he bade farewell to earth,
And went to live in Heaven.

Benjamin Yelland died 20 April 1862 aged 16 months.

PANCRASWEEK (ST PANCRAS)

Remov'd from every ill below,
Sweet and secure shall sleep,
His little heart no pain shall know,
His eyes no more shall weep.

Grave of George Thomas Jones son of Henry and Eliza Jones. Died 29th November 1857 aged 1 year and 8 months.

These two rather sentimental and genuinely pathetic verses represent a very commonly found Victorian genre; they would doubtless have been deplored by Augustus Hare (op.cit.) but probably gave much comfort to the grieving parents.

HOLSWORTHY (ST PETER AND ST PAUL)

Ah, lovely flower! Soon snatched away,
To bloom in realms divine:
Thousands will wish at Judgment day,
Their lives were short as thine.

Grave of Charles son of John and Betsey Parsons (of the Stanhope Arms Inn Holsworthy) who died 3rd December 1855 aged 5 years.

This gravestone also commemorates two other young children, Francis who died on 16th May 1858 aged 1 year 9 months and Charles Grigg Parsons who died on 23 rd August 1859 aged 3 years.

This example from Holsworthy seems especially strange to the modern reader. One cannot imagine many people wishing that their lives had been short, even if, as the text seems to imply they would have had time to sin more and thus be punished on Judgement Day!

NORTHLEW (ST THOMAS OF CANTERBURY)

Grave of Elizabeth Squire daughter of Jonas and Elizabeth Squire.
Died 17th April 1852, aged 5 years.

Here I must, sleep until doth come,
When all will have their final doom,
Ah! Thousands then will wish their time,
On earth had been so short as mine.

In the same mindset as the preceding Holsworthy example and possibly a 'pick n' mix' adaptation of the same original text. It is followed by a frequently found warning which implies that the reader may be next!

Reader behold and stop
One moment here and think,
I'm in Eternity,
And thou art on the brink.

LAMERTON (ST PETER)

Dear parents while on earth you dwell,
Weep not that I am gone before,
For though you lov'd me passing well,
My Lord, my Saviour, lov'd me more.

Grave of Susanna Gribble daughter of William and Susan Gribble. Died 16th October 1843 aged 5 years.

N.B. the above verse appears in Mogridge's book (op.cit.) as No.68 in amongst those recommended for 'Youth and Age'. A second verse, not included on Susanna's grave runs;

'twas he who call'd me up to heaven,
And not the Almighty's vengeful rod:
You could not give what he has given,
Nor guide and guard me like my God.

DUNTERTON (ALL SAINTS)

Parents weep not nor Brothers dear,
I am not dead but sleeping here:
Your grief for a temporal loss restrain,
We, in *Heav'n* I trust may meet again,
Farewell dear Friends & teachers too,
My school mates whom I love;
To all below I bid adieu,
To live with Christ above.

The grave of Elizabeth who was the only daughter of James and Elizabeth Fitze. She died on 22 September 1842 aged 14 years.

I cannot quite imagine these sentiments emanating from any children that I have ever taught!

NORTHLEW (ST THOMAS OF CANTERBURY)

Full fifteen months afflictions path I trod,
The appointed path to lead my soul to God;
When from on high the heavenly message came,
That bade me rise to bless my Saviour's name,
Kind parents all is well! Oh weep no more,
Rejoice to think my pains are o-er,
With joy celestial now your son is blest,
Prepare to follow to eternal rest.

Grave of Thomas Wood son of Thomas and Mary Wood 'of this village' Died 13th December 1839, aged 16.

This epitaph suggests that suffering from afflictions is a path to Heaven. Over the centuries some Christians have seen illnesses and other trials and tribulations as some kind of test sent by God. The sentiment that the departed's sufferings are over has long been and indeed remains a helpful one.

GREAT TORRINGTON (ST MICHAEL AND ALL ANGELS)

Towards the back of the nave a ledger stone marks the grave of a teenage girl:

Aged '14 Years and half'.

Does nature dictate not to mourn
Or blame a father's tears,
When from his heart's fond hope is torn,
The joy of early years.
Ah, no! it must be nature's voice,
Which speaks in ever'y vein;
Which bids ye Sons of mirth rejoice,
And woe indulge her pain
She's gone & her blest spirits fled
To happier realms, I trust,
Tho' here, entomb'd in earth's cold bed
Her relicks sleep in dust.

Grave of Emina Douglas Clinton the only daughter of W.D. Clinton. She died 20th September 1824.

The Clinton's were a family of some moment, possibly related to the local landowner Lord Clinton. The style of the epitaph is that favoured by the higher echelons of society.

NEWTON ST CYRES (ST CYR AND ST JULITTA)

This tablet commemorates Thomas the son of Sir John and Jane Quicke. He was seven years old at the time of his death. It seemed to me even at first glance that this was a much adored child and probably might have been a *prodigy* even allowing for the fact that his parents or family would in all probability have written this epitaph. It is placed where the public at large could see it, in a prominent position in the north aisle of the church:

His desire of Knowledge was so great.
And his Understanding so astonishing;
That he was deservedly loved, admir'd
And lamented By all who knew him

Such was his Genius, such his gifted Mind,
As seem'd to speak him, more than human kind;
Infant in Years yet so enlarg'd of Soul.
He grasp'd the Globe, and stretch'd from Pole to Pole.
Above this World he soar'd, the sacred Song
Swell'd his young Heart and tun'd his infant Tongue.
Heav'n saw him perfect, e'er race began
Heav'n saw him Angel e'er he number'd Man,
And jealous of the Snares the World might lay
In Mercy snatch'd him to the Realms of Day.

Research subsequently revealed two letters written by this little boy a few months prior to his death (3rd July 1771) when he was not yet eight years of age. These letters were written to his older brother who seems to have been away at school in the early spring, and these display above average intelligence and the best hand that I have seen any child write!

After Tom's death his mother Jane wrote a detailed account of her son's last days. Evidence suggests (for it states that *this is My dear Friend Mrs Raleigh's Copy of My account of My dear Thomas Quicke* ...(sic)) that there was once more than one copy of this account presumably written both for relatives and friends? The unusual nature of the boy is shown by the fact that he asked to have a history book read to him when he was in fact on his death bed!

The account ends with another poem which could equally well have been Tom's epitaph and suggests that it was probably Jane his mother who had written the epitaph in the church. It runs:

...& May I The Mother of so Sweet a child
His false imagin'd loss cease to lament
And wisely curb thy sorrows wild

Think what a present I to God have sent
And render him with patience what he lent

Within his Heart did ev'ry Virtue dwell
His sparkling Eyes were like the Orient beam

In each just Attribute he did excel
And true proportion harmoniz'd his frame

In manners lively, Great in Mind
By Nature open and Sincere

TAWSTOCK (ST PETER)

Affixed to one of the pillars which support the tower is this memorial plaque dedicated to 14 year old Joan Lovet who died in 1679. She was the daughter of Edward Lovet Esq. and his wife Joan.

She Liv'd A few Yeares only to show,
How Soon Grace Might unto Perfection Grow
The Virgin Robe was Ready, and she Cry'd
I come I come, Sweet Jesu and Soe Dy'd.
His Understanding Solid, Quick, & Clear.

PETER TAVY (ST PETER)

Under this stone by natures fatall doome
Five sisters lie cropt in their tender bloome
They breathed awhile, and lokt ye world about
And like new lighted candles soone went out
Their sunne noe sooner did arise, but set.
Their journies end, at setting forth they met
They op'd their eyes, and in the worlds disdaine
Full quicklie did they close them up againe
Their life was short the lesse they did amisse
The shorter life the longer is their blisse

Five infant sisters, from one wombe
Here lie together in one tombe
Their tyde did ebb, before full sea
Their welcome was their well a way
Their parents have noe cause to weepe
Sith they lie here but in a sleep.

Dated September 1632 this slate once covered the mortal remains of the daughters of the Reverend Richard Evelegh the rector of Peter Tavy. An inscription also tells us that these children were two named Marie, two named Elizabeth and one called Eleonor. I assume that *Sith* is the modern *since.*

A typical Victorian headstone in the Dolvin Road Cemetery, Tavistock.

During the later twentieth century many churchyards were cleared of headstones to facilitate grass cutting. At Tavistock (St Eustachius) most have been re-sited back to back close to the vestry and are luckily both in good condition and easily readable.

This coffin-shaped table tomb is found on the south side of Walkhampton churchyard. The departed *Mr William Shillibear was the local schoolmaster who died on 4th June 1827 aged 71. In such affection was he held that according to his epitaph, his funeral was attended '…by upwards of 1500 persons…' the majority of which were '…uninvited…' He whilst '…living was beloved.' (and) '…In death revered.'*

St Sidwell's church in Exeter was destroyed in the Blitz of 4th May 1942; the churchyard with its tombs and headstones was also devastated. Some surviving stones are placed around the perimeter walls.

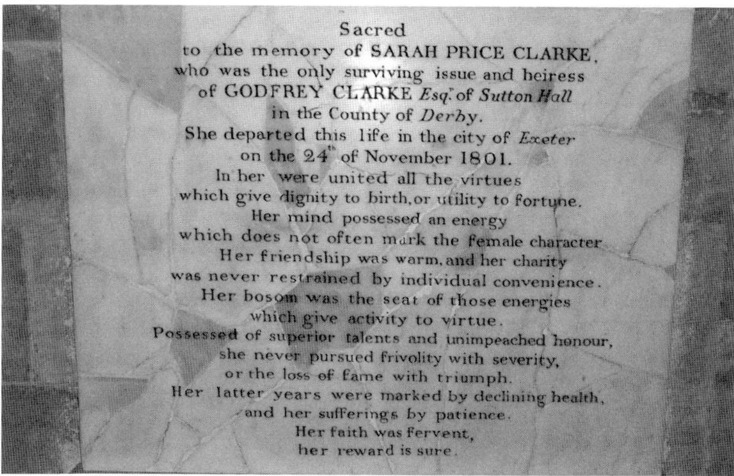

Sacred
to the memory of SARAH PRICE CLARKE,
who was the only surviving issue and heiress
of GODFREY CLARKE Esq.r of Sutton Hall
in the County of Derby.
She departed this life in the city of Exeter
on the 24th of November 1801.
In her were united all the virtues
which give dignity to birth, or utility to fortune.
Her mind possessed an energy
which does not often mark the female character
Her friendship was warm, and her charity
was never restrained by individual convenience.
Her bosom was the seat of those energies
which give activity to virtue.
Possessed of superior talents and unimpeached honour,
she never pursued frivolity with severity,
or the loss of fame with triumph.
Her latter years were marked by declining health,
and her sufferings by patience.
Her faith was fervent,
her reward is sure.

This marble plaque which is to be found in the south quire aisle of Exeter Cathedral was lucky to survive the Blitz being situated on the wall that was all but flattened when a high explosive *bomb fell outside. In common with this plaque many were badly damaged but later restored.*

Sacred to the Memory
of RACHEL CHARLOTTE O'BRIEN,
Wife of Capt. E. J. O'BRIEN
of his Majesty's 24th Regt.
and Daughter of JOS. FROBISHER Esq.
of Montreal, Canada.
Her Death was occasioned
by her Clothes catching Fire;
seeing the Flames
communicating to her Infant,
all Regard to her own Safety,
was lost in the
more powerful Consideration
of saving her Child,
and rushing
out of the Room, she
preserved its Life, at the
Sacrifice of her own.
She expired on the 13th of Dec.
A.D. 1800,
in the 19th Year of her Age.

This poignant epitaph can be found in the north quire aisle of Exeter Cathedral.

Lydford churchyard has many eighteenth-century slate headstones, both with and without epitaphs.

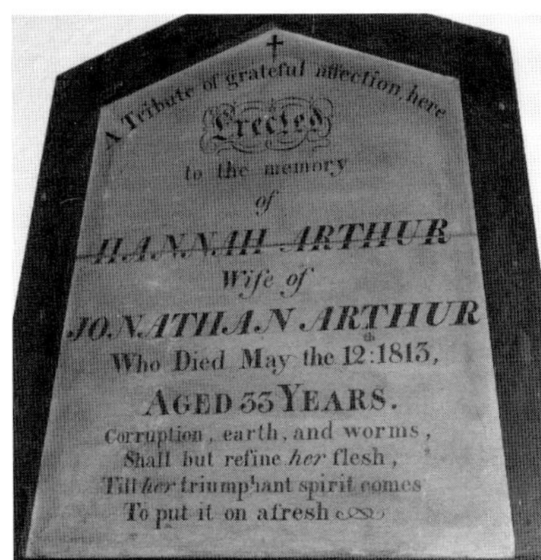

Above: *This memorial which is in Peter Tavy church is unusual in that it is constructed of wooden boards. This was a normal medium for Royal Coats of Arms, details of parochial charities or listing the Ten Commandments but was (one suspects) employed as an inexpensive alternative to marble or slate in this case.*

Below: *In many churches across England the Royal Coat of Arms can still be found. Occasionally these are of plaster but normally as here at Gittisham, painted on boards.*

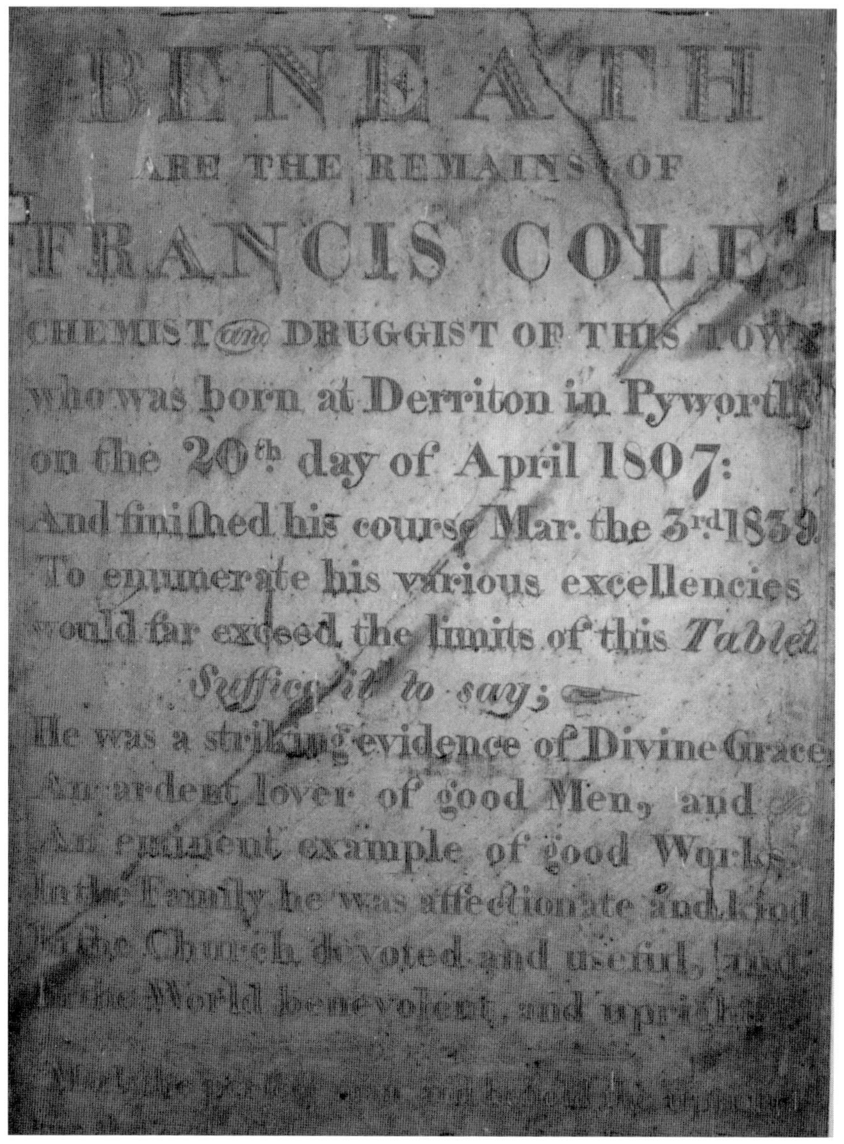

BENEATH
ARE THE REMAINS OF
FRANCIS COLE
CHEMIST and DRUGGIST OF THIS TOW
who was born at Derriton in Pyworth
on the 20th day of April 1807:
And finished his course Mar. the 3rd 1839.
To enumerate his various excellencies
would far exceed the limits of this Tablet
Suffice it to say;
He was a striking evidence of Divine Grace,
An ardent lover of good Men, and
An eminent example of good Works.
In the Family he was affectionate and kind
In the Church devoted and useful, and
In the World benevolent, and upright

Although found affixed to the south inside wall of Holsworthy church this is clearly a headstone from the churchyard, possibly damaged by the falling of a tree and long ago brought into the church for preservation.

Occasionally older and in this case often illegible headstones are employed as edging for churchyard paths. (Drewsteignton).

Sadly lying on its back at the edge of the churchyard, but otherwise in pristine condition. (Drewsteignton).

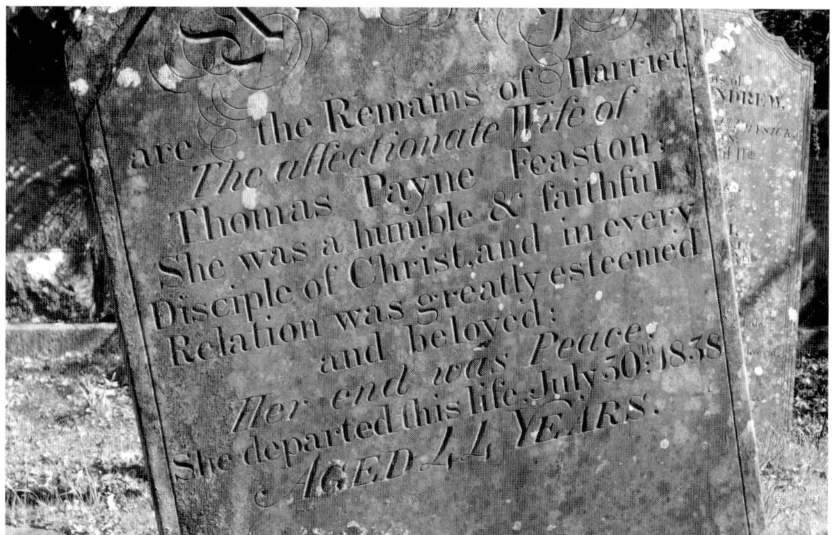

Lying at a picturesque angle, the headstone of Harriet Payne. Dolvin Road Cemetery Tavistock.

This epitaph embossed on an iron plaque is not found in either churchyard nor public cemetery but on Dartmoor in a spot favoured by the departed. (Highdown Lydford).

EPITAPHS FOR THOSE WHO DIED PREMATURELY IN EARLY ADULT LIFE

CREDITON (HOLY CROSS)

On the wall of the south aisle is a memorial erected in 1946 to two young men who died on active service in the R.A.F. during the Second World War. Although of modern design the literary style of the epitaph is not so far removed from those of earlier times:

LET THEIR DEATHS REMIND THOSE WHO COME AFTER
AT HOW GREAT A PRICE IS FREEDOM PURCHASED.

LET IT ALSO BE REMEMBERED THAT 'IN SMALL
PROPORTIONS WE JUST BEAUTIES SEE, AND
THAT IN SHORT MEASURES LIFE MAY PERFECT BE.'

The quotation is taken from a work written by Ben Jonson (1572-1637).

LYDFORD
(MEMORIAL FOUND NOT IN THE CHURCH BUT AT HIGHDOWN)

This memorial which is found on the north-west edge of Dartmoor is in the form of an iron plaque affixed to some rocks overlooking the river Lyd and Wiggery Tor with its stone cross on the summit. It commemorates Captain Nigel Duncan Ratcliffe Hunter M.C. (Bar) who was killed in action on 25th March 1918 at Biefvillers near Bapaume. He was 23 years old and had written this poem during his last visit to Lydford.

ARE WE NOT LIKE THIS MOORLAND STREAM
SPRINGING NONE KNOWS WHERE FROM,

TINKLING, BUBBLING, FLASHING A GLEAM BACK AT THE SUN:
E'ER LONG GLOOMY AND DULL, UNDER A CLOUD:
THEN RUSHING ONWARDS AGAIN:
DASHING AT ROCKS WITH ANGER LOUD,
ROARING AND FOAMING IN VAIN?
WANDERING THUS FOR MANY A MILE,
TWISTING AND TURNING AWAY FOR A WHILE,
THEN OF A SUDDEN 'TIS OVER THE FALL
AND THE DARK STILL POOL IS THE END OF ALL.

IS IT? I THOUGHT AS I TURNED AWAY:
AND I TURNED AGAIN TO THE SILENT MOOR,
IS IT? I SAID, AND MY HEART SAID "NAY"!
AS I GAZED AT THE CROSS ON "WIDGERY TOR."

N.B. Captain Hunter is buried in France; his name is also remembered on the memorial at Beaulencourt British Cemetery in the Pas de Calais.

BOVEY TRACEY
(ST PETER, ST PAUL AND ST THOMAS OF CANTERBURY)

A brass plaque on the wall of the south aisle commemorates Havilland Chepmell Vere Stead one-time Assistant District Governor at Axian. He died at Kromokrum in what was then the Gold Coast Colony (now Ghana) on 2nd May 1902 aged 27. His epitaph reads;

A SOUL GOES OUT ON THE EAST WIND
WHO DIED FOR ENGLAND'S SAKE

This line is taken from the middle of a verse found in Rudyard Kipling's longish poem entitled *The English Flag*. To put it a little more in context the preceding line runs: '*Never the lotus closes, never the wild-fowl wakes…*'

PANCRASWEEK (ST PANCRAS)

Nipt by the wind's unkindly blast,
Parched by the suns director ray,
The momentary glories waste,
The short lived beauties die away.

Grave of Jane Moore the wife of Mark Moore. She died 16th July 1889, aged 27 years.

This poem also appears at nearby Launcells (Cornwall) on the gravestone of another young woman, 23 year old Elizabeth Ann Hambly who died at Plymouth on 24th November 1898. Interestingly the source for the lines is in fact the second verse of the hymn *'The morning flowers display their sweets'* taken presumably from a then recent (1890) revision of Wesley's *A collection of hymns for the people called Methodists* first published in London in 1780. The text is based on Isaiah 40 verses 6-8 and also appeared in the U.S.A. in the Hymnbook of the Protestant Episcopal Press as Hymn No. 205 published in 1835, so the lines were well- known in the wider English-speaking World. Sources www.ccel.org.w/wesley/hymn, and www.books.google.com.

BELSTONE (ST MARY)

Day after day we saw them fade,
And gently pass away,
and after in our hearts we prayed
that they might longer stay.

Grave of William Reddaway who died 23rd June 1891 aged 19 and his sister Sarah who died on 26th November 1893 aged 24.

This is an example of Victorian funerary verse that can be readily adapted by the change of personal pronouns, e.g '...we saw her/him fade....' . Whilst I have not been able to trace the original source I have noted that these lines were used in the *In Memoriam* section of at least one newspaper in the U.K. during the 1990s.

TAWSTOCK (ST PETER)

How short was the warning that called me away,
How soon my soul blasted my bones now decay,
All these that survives prepair for the call,
For God only knows the next that may fall.

The grave of Sarah Smaldon aged 25 years daughter of James and Mary Smaldon who died 18th December 1848.

This typical nineteenth century verse deals with two themes very common in funerary verse during both the eighteenth and nineteenth centuries; the ideas of death coming without warning and thus the need for those left to be ready in case they are next!

CORYTON (ST ANDREW)

Sudden from this transient state he fled
One day in health the next among the dead
Reader consider well how short a span
And how uncertain is the life of man
Therefore dear friends grief not for me in vain
In Heaven I would all shall meet again.

Grave of Thomas Cumming, died 16th August 1844 aged 38.

The message of this poem is much the same as the previous example. Take care!

NORTHLEW (ST THOMAS OF CANTERBURY)

O Gay and thoughtless ponder here,
And do not serious things defer:
Death from his mission will not stay,
But soon will hurry you away.

Grave of Charlotte Cole wife of Samuel Cole.

Died 27th December 1836, aged 30.

The theme continues; don't waste your life on amusements. Younger readers should remember that gay meant joyful, fun loving and colourful until a few decades ago!

EXETER (ST MARTIN)

The monument is in memory of Eliza Mary Mortimer aged 16 who died on 6th June 1826.

As a Christian, she was humble and devout;
As a child, dutiful and affectionate;
As a relative and friend, kind and sincere;

Whilst her purity of mind,
And benevolence of heart obtained universal regard & esteem.

This early promise of future excellence, the almighty in his inscrutable
wisdom saw fit to blight 'ere the blossom could be matured,
And 'tho' for a long period heavily afflicted by the hand of providence,
She endured her acute sufferings with the meekest resignation,
And bent submissively to the divine decree,
Supported and animated by the firmest hope of reposing in the
bosom of her saviour and her God.

Eliza was the only child of Samuel and Elizabeth Mortimer who both lived into their eighties.

Often eighteenth and nineteenth century epitaphs credit those they commemorate with dying well. The confident belief in Heaven would have been very widely held. Epitaphs of this sort are invariably unique in their exact wording although would have been influenced by the fashions and sentiments of the day and no doubt by the bereaved having had sight of similar wording.

TAVISTOCK (ST EUSTACHIUS)

Sadly virtually all the gravestones were cleared from their original locations at some time during the twentieth century, presumably to make grass-cutting easier; so we cannot know where in the churchyard the subject of these lines now lies. The stones are all neatly assembled in lines close to the south side of the church.

Francis Lovis was the son of Francis and Elizabeth Lovis and he died on 5th August 1826 at the age of 21. There are vague allusions to the manner of his death in the poem:

Again the monster *Death*
Hath seiz'd his youthful prey;
With sudden violence stopp'd the breath
And forc'd the soul away.
Lately we saw him here.
Amongst the social band
How well, how blithe did he appear
No evil seem'd at hand
But to that very eve,
The fierce affliction came
You would the feeble body leave.
Till quite dissolv'd his frame,
Third succeeding day
The mortal strife was done:
Death triumphed o'er the breathless day
Before the setting sun
O Youth be wise in time
Make GOD your only friend
To him devote your blooming prime
Then peace shall be your end.

Clearly these lines are original, but whether they describe dying as the result of some accident or more likely the sudden onset of a disease such as cholera one cannot say.

CHITTLEHAMPTON (ST HIERITHA)

William Rendle's gravestone is close to the south porch of this large village church. He died, his headstone tells us, after a long and painful illness aged 23 years on 22nd November 1817.
A mixture of Roman script and italics it reads:

Here lies a young Man who without pretence
Was blest with reason and with sober sense
Pride and passion were to his soul unknown
Virtue's bright beams perfectly in him shone
And tho' his body is mouldering in the dust,
His soul we hope is numbered with the blest.
Let us his bright Example keep in view,
And to this worlds allurements bid adieu
Let us our hearts to nether mansions rise
And fix our thoughts on things beyond the skies.

ASHBURTON (ST ANDREW)

A marble plaque in the church commemorates the life of Thomas Bonner Cousins the son of Thomas and Ann Cousins. He died on 12th February 1815 aged but 17 years.

Here lies – divested of his cumb'rous Clay,
A youth – sincere – affectionate and kind:
His dawn of Life to Virtue led the way.
And useful Learning grac'd his early Mind.
Short was his transient Life,
Just sent to raise,
Th' aspiring hopes, then leave us to deplore,
His thread of Life spun out,
the airy Blaze,
Shone for a Moment,
and was seen no more
Thrice happy Youth!
O what Fate was Thine.
Calmly to pass thro' this dark vale of Tears;

Destin'd so soon Life's Burden to resign.
So soon translated to the heavenly spheres.

N.B. the line 'Thrice happy Youth!' Possibly suggests a reference to the book *Alonzo or The Youthful Solitaire* (Pub. J.Robson, London 1772).

SHUTE (ST MICHAEL)

Sophia Anne was the wife of Sir William Templer Pole Bart.
She died aged 20 on 17th March 1803. She as her memorial tells us:

...had issue one Daughter and two Sons

SOPHIA ANNE, born June 11th 1805.
Died September 3rd 1805
WILLIAM TEMPLER, born June 12th 1806
And JOHN GEORGE, born January 21st 1808
Whose birth she survived only a few weeks...

Her epitaph is an excellent example of the bespoke poetry which the upper levels of Georgian society could produce:

Could Love connubial, or parental care,
Or Art, the ravage of disease repair;
Could Youth and Innocence, or Virtue free
From Heavens all wise howe'er severe decree,
Thou hadst not fall'in in Beauty's Morning bloom,
Death's early prey, the tenant of the Tomb:
Still had thy Spirit, pure as light supplied
The joys that with thee liv'd that with thee died.
Here reader! Pause and though this Marble tell
How prematurely Youth and Beauty fell:

While sympathising Pity mourns her lot.
Be neither Christian Faith, nor Hope forgot.
Though Memory oft, at Nature's dictate turn.
With tears and sighs to dear SOPHIA's Urn
They who best knew and therefore lov'd her most

To this world only deem as Angel lost:
And trust the day will come when borne sublime
Alike beyond the reach of Death and Time,
They too amidst eternal joys, shall dwell
With her they mourn so much and lov'd so well.

CULLOMPTON (ST ANDREW)

The monument to the three Coleman boys, notably of Augustus aged 21 and his fifteen year old brother who both died in the year 1795, has already been referred to in the introductory sections. Their epitaph if such it is, is a case of what the parents *hoped for*! It runs:

This monument is erected to perpetuate the Memory of two excellent Youths, who had it pleased God to have spared their Lives, would have been Ornaments to their Professions and their Country.

LAMERTON (ST PETER)

Weep not for me it is in vain
Your lost is my Eternal gain
For old and young all that have breath
When God seeth fit must stupe to death

Grave of Sarah the wife of Robert Bickell who was buried on 19th March 1774 aged 29 years.

This seems to be a run of the mill verse, inscribed many decades before it could have been plagiarised from some anthology of verse. Death is inevitable!

LAMERTON (ST PETER)

Our Bodys in this grave must lie,
In silence till the Judgement Day
My Husband and my children dear
Prepare for death for to lie here
Weep no lament for us nomore

We are not lost but gone before
And we shall rise at Christ's call
To dwell with Saints and Angels all.

The above verse is best understood in the context of the genealogical detail also inscribed on the gravestone:

'Here Lieth the Body of Mary the Wife of Thomas Rice who was buried ye 27th day of December 1770 Aged 28 years.

Also two daughters of Thomas Rice and Mary his Wife , Ann there Daughter was buried ye 28th day of August 1770 Aged 10 months.

Mary their Daughter was buried ye 22nd day of October 1772 Aged 5 years.'

DUNTERTON (ALL SAINTS)

My Glass was quickly run.
My days did swiftly fly.
Like to a tale that is began.
And ended by & by.

James Neale aged 38, was buried shortly after Christmas on 29th December 1753.

His life is likened to an hour glass.

NORTHLEW (ST THOMAS OF CANTERBURY)

Tho sudden death with his unerring dart
When immature didst pierce my tender hart
Yet it hath only sent my Flesh to dust
To lift my soul to Heav'n with Saints and just
Weep not for me my Friends and parents dear
Tis God's decree and his parental care
Hath nipt me just full grown which doth presage
How weak is youth and how much weaker age.

Grave of Elizabeth daughter of Nicholas & Elizabeth Wood.
Died 14th September 1751, 'in the 21st year of her age'.

The metaphor *unerring dart* possibly taken from Homer's *Iliad.*

BRANSCOMBE (ST WINIFRED)

On a slate wall plaque on the south side of the church are these lines:

In Christ, I liv'd, and dy'd,
Through him, to live again;
What's vile, in Life have left,
In hopes, with Him to, Reign.

The departed was Mrs Anne Churchill aged 23 who died on 7th November 1741.

TAVISTOCK (ST EUSTACHIUS)

Elizabeth the daughter of Roger and Judith Edwards was buried on 13th January 1739, she was 18 years of age.

WHY should not tender parents cease to grieve.
And my departure teach them how to live.
Or why should friends lament & sisters cry.
Tis Gods Decree all that are born must dye.
Make his most holy laws your chiefest care
And for a blest Eternity prepare.
That you (with me) may Hallelujahs sing.
Sorrows adieu: Blest be our Glorious King.

Again, death is inevitable, it is God's will. We will meet again!

PAIGNTON (ST JOHN)

In memory of '…JOAN BUTLAND and son who died in childbed y 9th day of November 1679.'

In Night of death, here rests ye good &
fair, who all life Day, gave God both heart
and ear, no Dirt, nor Distance, hinder'd
he Resort, for love still paved y way, &
cut it short, to parents, husband, friends
none Better knew, ye tribute of dvty &
she paid it tow. Beloved By & loving
all Dearly, her son to whom she
first gave life, then lost her owne
he kind poor lamb for his Dam a full
year cried, alas in vain, ther for, for
Love he died.

This sad tale speaks very much for itself.
N.B. 4th line *he* = *his*
7th line *tow* = too
10th line *Dam* = mother

TAWSTOCK (ST PETER)

Mary the daughter of Miles Baron and his wife Ann died in '…the flower of her age…' as her ledger stone states:

She to ye Lamb her Bridegroom hasted hence
Clad in ye pure white robe of innocence
Her parents thought to match her here;
But She would only unto Christ espoused be
To mourn for her Virginity forbear
Twas her desire a Virgin Crowne to weare
Like ye wise Virgins well prepar'd was
And now her Lamp shines to Eternitie.

She died 13th January 1679.

N.B. '...to ye Lamb her Bridegroom hasted hence...' The Lamb in Christian theology means Christ known as *The Lamb of God* commonly seen in Christian iconography. The idea of Christ as the bridegroom is not unheard of, Roman Catholic nuns being thought of as brides of Christ in a spiritual sense and thus when taking their vows place a ring on their wedding finger.

It seems that the young lady was to have been married? The Wise Virgins referred to are those five who in St Matthew's Gospel 25:1-13 have sufficient oil in their lamps and go to meet the Bridegroom (who stands for Christ in the story), as opposed to the five who were *not* ready because they had insufficient oil. This is a parable about being ready for Christ. Here it implies that she was both pure and ready to meet God. e.g. to die prepared.

EXMINSTER (ST MARTIN)

Buried in a small vault under the flooring of this church lay the mortal remains of a young wife. Grace the daughter of Henry Tothill (the then Sheriff of Devon) had already married William Tothill Esq. (presumably a cousin?) of the Middle Temple when she met an untimely end at the age of 17 on 24th February 1623. Her epitaph runs:

IF GRACE COULD LENGTHE OF DAYES YE GIVE OR VERTUE
COULD THEE HERE HAVE KEPT
OR TEARES OF FRINDES WHICH FOR THEE WEPT
THEN HAD'ST THOU LIVD AMONGST US HEERE
TO WHOM THY VERTUES MADE THEE DEER
BUT THOU A SAINTE DID'ST HEAVEN ASPIRE
WHILES HEERE ON EARTH WEE THEE ADMIRE
THEN REST DEERE CORPS IN MANTLE CLAYE
TILL CHRIST THEE RAISE THE LATTER DAY

Beneath this inscription is added:

THY YERES WERE FEWE THY GLASSE BEINGE RUNN
WHERE DEATH DID ENDE THY LYFE BEGUNN (SIC)

N.B. In this case I have departed from my usual practice of rendering the transcription exactly; in order to make the poem flow for the modern reader I have taken the liberty of using the letter u where the original has used the v which was at the time written for both u *and* v. I have not altered the text in any other way.

'THE LATTER DAY' = *THE LAST DAY* otherwise Judgement Day when in Christian eschatology Christ will return to judge both the living and the dead.

EPITAPHS FOR THOSE WHO DIED IN THE PRIME OF LIFE

As a general rule I have included in this section all those who departed this life between the ages of thirty and fifty nine years.

TAWSTOCK (ST PETER)

Captain William Bourchier Sherard Wrey C.M.G. C.B.E. is commemorated on one of the many plaques to be found in this church. He died on 6th January 1926 aged 59 His plaque tell us that he was present at the Relief of Peking (this would be at the time of the Boxer Uprising in 1900) and that he had also seen service in Egypt. I have included his epitaph which although a biblical one taken from Numbers Chapter 20 verse 17 seems obscure to the casual reader. It runs:

'We will go by the Kings Highway, we will not turn to the right hand nor to the left until we have passed thy borders.'

In fact I discovered that 'The Kings Highway' is a name anciently given to a trade route which ran from Heliopolis in northern Egypt via Suez, across Sinai to Aqaba, from thence it ran through Jordan close to Petra and via Amman to Resafa on the upper Euphrates where it ended. Knowing that the departed had served in Egypt in 1882 and 1885 the choice of verse with no doubt the inference of his keeping to the straight and narrow path is perhaps more readily understood. It may even refer to some specific act in the life of the departed.

BUCKFASTLEIGH (HOLY TRINITY)

N.B. The church is now sadly in ruins having been largely destroyed by fire in 1992.

Do not ask us if we miss her,
There is such a vacant place,
Can we e'er forget her footsteps
And that dear familiar face.

Found on the gravestone of Emily Jane Wood wife of Walter Wood who died 7th April 1915 aged 50.

Also included here is a variant version of what was clearly an easily adapted poem taken from an undertaker's book which I also noted on the gravestone of Elizabeth Ann Hambly at Launcells (Cornwall) who was buried in 1898. This verse could be varied in case the departed should be a man by changing the personal pronouns; thus at Bridestowe I saw the headstone of John Henry Kellaway who died on 22nd August 1914 aged 45.

Do not ask if we miss him
There is such a vacant place
We shall never forget his footsteps
Nor his dear familiar face

EXETER (ST DAVID)

Suddenly I was called hence.
It was the will of Providence.
May Those whom I have left behind.
His grace and goodness ever find.

Grave of Frederick Henry Tucker. Died 9th April 1904, aged 27 years.

LYDFORD (ST PETROC)

I first saw the verse which follows at Lydford, on the headstone of George Powell who died on 2nd Feb. 1910 at the age of 32.

Long days and nights he bore his pain, To think of rest was all in vain, Until the Lord he thought it best, To cease his pain and give him rest.

These lines must however come from a printed source as I later discovered the existence of a variant version in the Presbyterian Cemetery at Grenfel in New South Wales:

In loving memory of
Walter Ingrey
Born at Ashwell, Hertfordshire, England
13th Aug 1838
Died at Grenfell 10th may 1916
Long days and nights he bore in pain
to wait for cure was all in vain
but God above, who thought it best
did ease his pain and give him rest

Source: rootsweb.com

The next poem is surely one of the most ubiquitous of all graveyard verses in this *Prime of Life* section because the wording made it appeal to the whole spectrum of the bereaved thus it was suitable for young, middle-aged and old alike.

The cup was bitter, the sting severe. To part with one we love so dear.
The trial is hard we'll not complain. But trust in Christ to meet again.

This was clearly a very popular verse. I found the same at Lydford (St Petroc) for Richard Blamey d. 14th June 1885, aged 54. For Bessie Combes who died 20th April 1889 aged 12 at Holsworthy (St Peter and St Paul). Also at Gulworthy (St Paul) for John Down aged 68, who died 27th April 1896. At Bridestowe (St Bridget) for Bessie Hockaday died 24th April 1906 age 35. Likewise found just across the Tamar at St Stephen, Launceston (Cornwall), on the grave of Mary the wife of John Poolew (sic) who died 3rd December 1889 aged 26. The lines clearly come from a published source that was available throughout the English-speaking world since they can even be found on the grave of Rose Gregory (née Gasper) died 22nd March 1912, in the Lower Circular Road Cemetery in Calcutta, India. (Source: www.rootsweb.com)

LYDFORD (ST PETROC)

I first came upon these lines at Lydford

Not gone from memory, not gone from love,
but gone to her father's home above.

for Ann Hooper late of Holsworthy who died 29th Nov 1897 aged 77.

But this is clearly another widely used and easily adapted published verse and again appropriate to many situations. I noted it also at Hoath (Holy Cross) in Kent on the grave of a 76 year old and in India (Lower Circular Road Cemetery op.cit.) and at the Church of England Cemetery at Grenfel New South Wales in a variant form:

In memory of
Esther Ingrey
died May 4 1880
aged 4 years
and 6 months
Not gone from memory
not gone from love
but gone to a better
love above.

Source: rootsweb.com

LAMERTON (ST PETER)

The gravestone of Henry Vicars (a miner) who died 20th January 1865, has a somewhat bizarre choice of epitaph especially when one discovers the origins of the lines: written circa 1803 they were in fact the first half of an epitaph for an Irish patriot named Robert Emnet who was hung for treason after an abortive attack on Dublin Castle in 1803. Written by one Thomas More (1780-1852) they were subsequently set to music and sung as a ballard in Ireland! One wonders whether those who commissioned this inscription and indeed the parson knew of the origins of this piece?

Oh! Breathe not his name;
Let it sleep in the shade,
Where cold and lamented,
His relics are laid.

Sad, silent and dark,
Be the tears that we shed,
As the night dew, that falls,
On the grass, o'er his head.

BUDLEIGH SALTERTON (METHODIST CHURCH)

This fascinating epitaph is found on a wall plaque adjacent to what is nowadays a social and refreshment area in the church.

> TO RESUE FROM OBLIVION THE REVERED MEMORY OF THE REV.D LEWIS LEWIS MINISTER OF THE GOSPEL IN THE WESLEYAN BRANCH OF CHRIST'S CHURCH MILITANT HERE ON EARTH THIS TABLET IS ERECTED BY HIS SORROWING FLOCK IN SALTERTON, OVER WHOM HE WAS THE FAITHFUL PASTOR.
>
> AS A MISSIONARY IN THE WEST INDIES, AND AS A MINISTER AT HOME, HE SERVED GOD IN HIS DAY AND GENERATION WITH MUCH FIDELITY AND USEFULNESS, AND WAS THEN CALLED TO HIS ETERNAL REST BY A MYSTERIOUS PROVIDENCE, IN THE MIDST OF LIFE, THE 24TH JUNE 1848, IN THE 35TH YEAR OF HIS AGE.

N.B. The terms Wesleyan and Methodist are synonymous.

CHRIST'S CHURCH MILITANT HERE ON EARTH, is an apt phrase taken the Communion service in the Anglican Book of Common Prayer (1662).The phrase 'IN THE MIDST OF LIFE' is taken from the same source and is an extract from burial service which famously continues '…we are in death…' Methodist liturgy, especially in former times, closely followed Anglican practice from which church it is of course descended.

PETER TAVY (ST PETER)

An unexpected stroke,
When none was near to save;
My thread of being broke,
And brought me to the grave,
Then thou who knows't my fate,
While pondering o'er this sod,
As short may be thy days,
Prepare to meet thy God.

Grave of William Rice aged 42 who died 6th February 1841.

The modern reader should not assume that stroke here means an infarction but merely whatever action of God or man ended this man's life. A ubiquitous theme here. The message is clear: *Prepare to meet thy God!*

WALKHAMPTON (ST MARY THE VIRGIN)

Not fierce disease alone, or slow decay,
Or vile intemperance, sweep mankind away.
Oft the busiest hour when health is high,
And sin itself is distant, death nigh.
One blow shall send the living to the dead,
Or lay him ling'ring on his last sick bed
Soon to yield up his soul!
Such lot was mine.
Reader beware it may be also thine!
Repent. Return to Christ and keep his way
Then shalt thou live prepared from day to day.

Grave of Alexander Frayne Seargent who died 14th May 1840.

The oft repeated theme, be prepared!

TAVISTOCK (ST EUSTACHIUS)

O the Grave! While it covers each fault, each defect,

Leaves untarnish'd the worth of the just;
And her memory is cherish'd with tender respect,
While her body consumes in the dust.

Grace Snell aged 54 is commemorated by these words. The wife of the late John Snell, she died on 8th May 1829.

TOTNES (ST MARY)

Caroline Taunton the wife of William Doige Taunton a Totnes solicitor died on 6th July 1827. According to her epitaph;

She was an example worthy of imitation in all the varied relations of female life; and the graces of her mind, and the beauty of her person were surpassed only by her Christian Piety, an ornament to her Sex, and a blessing to her Family.

Having for a period of fourteen years discharged the duties of a Wife and Mother; with tender solicitude and conscientious fidelity, she fell a patient victim; in the flower of her age, to a lingering and hopeless disease, leaving three Sons and three Daughters, whose infancy she had trained in the paths of virtue, and religion, to weep over her early Grave….

During the eighteenth century and through much of the nineteenth the professional and upper classes generated a considerable volume of similar epitaphs, frequently referring to the piety and to the seemingly faultless lives of the deceased.

TAVISTOCK (ST EUSTACHIUS)

Alas she's gone just past the prime of life,
A Husband fond has lost a loving Wife,
Dissolv'd at once are natures dearest ties,
Lo in the dust a prey for worms she lies,
Till the Trump calls her to those realms above,
To meet her Saviour & her God of love.

Gravestone of Mary the wife of John Martin. She died 22nd June 1826 aged 54 years. Her husband was interred in the same grave and his details added after *his* death on 29th October 1836 aged 63 years.

N.B. 'the trump' is of course a reference to the trumpet calls which will herald the Last Day or Judgement Day when the departed will be woken from their slumbers for the Final Judgement. The reference to being prey for worms might be thought a little indelicate by some, but is of course a matter of fact and was an idea quite frequently expressed in epitaphs prior to the twentieth century. It is perhaps used to make the point that it is a person's spirit *not* the body which will enjoy the afterlife.

It is perhaps worth noting that in the creeds used by both the Anglican and Roman Catholic Churches that a belief in '...resurrection of the body...' is expressed. The creeds were composed over 1500 years ago and although these words are recited day by day the belief very widely held nowadays is in a spiritual resurrection. It is also worth stating that when these epitaphs were written the great majority of people thought of Heaven as a paradise in the sky, hence the use of terms such as '...to those realms above...' A further issue which presents something of a dichotomy is the concept of what is almost two parallel beliefs. Some epitaphs expressing the idea that one will slumber in one's grave until Judgement Day and then rise; whereas others may convey the belief that the dead are already in Heaven. This is a dichotomy of belief which still prevails in some quarters.

EXMINSTER (ST MARTIN)

I have avoided quoting the ubiquitous passages from the Bible which appear almost in equal numbers on the memorial plaques of the rich and the gravestones of lesser mortals. What is far less often found, indeed I would say that it was unusual, is a quotation from the Anglican Church's *Book of Common Prayer*, which with modifications in 1552 and 1662 has been in use since the year 1549.

On the memorial plaque dedicated to Samuel Kekewich Esq. who died 26th August 1822 aged 56 years, in addition to a quotation from Psalm 25, we read:

Give us grace so to follow their good examples, that with them we may be partakers of thy heavenly kingdom.

This is taken from the Prayer for the Church Militant, composed by Thomas Cranmer. It is from the part of the Communion service which follows the Offertory. Rightly it should not start with the capital G but as the writer of the epitaph has understandably made an extract into a stand-alone sentence I have quoted it so.

WALKHAMPTON (ST MARY THE VIRGIN)

Consumption dreadful struck his inward blow,
The stroke was certain but the effect was slow
With wasting pains, Death saw me sore opprest
Pity'd my sighs, and kindly gave me rest.

Grave of John Kinsman who died 26th August 1815 aged 46 years.

This verse also appears at North Tawton near Okehampton where it forms the first half of a longer poem. It is probably reasonable to assume that consumption here indicates T.B., a disease that was then endemic and although more likely to effect those who lived in crowded and unhealthy conditions often struck at people of all classes. The words 'the effect was slow' would seem to confirm this. In Europe as a whole consumption may have accounted for around one in seven of all deaths during the nineteenth century, in crowded cities such as Paris the figure was at one time around 33%.

PETER TAVY (ST PETER)

Hannah the wife of Jonathan Arthur who died 12th May 1813 aged 33.

Corruption, earth, and worms,
Shall but refine *her* flesh,
Till *her* triumphant spirit comes,
To put it on afresh.

Whilst there is nothing especially unusual about the words here, there was one thing which made this plaque in Peter Tavy church out of the ordinary; it is not made of any kind of stone but is painted on boards with a wooden frame. Whilst this medium is not out of place in a church, being often used for lists of clergy or of an individual, charitable gifts, for the Royal Coats of Arms and often in bell towers to record successful 'peals', wood is not often used for this purpose.

TAVISTOCK (ST EUSTACHIUS)

HER PATIENCE AND RESIGNATION IN A LINGERING ILLNESS AND COMPOSURE AT THE HOUR OF DEATH EVINC'D WHAT REWARDS,
IN THE HEAVIEST AFFLICTIONS CHRISTIANITY ENSURES EVEN ON EARTH, FOR THE UNIFORM DISCHARGE OF THE SILENT AND MODEST VIRTUES OF FILIAL DUTY, CHARITY, FRIENDSHIP, CONJUGAL AFFECTION, AND EARLY PIETY.

This mural plaque which is in the north aisle of the church commemorates Mary Sleeman the wife of Captain Sleeman. She died on 9th October 1803.

Here Mary Sleeman is accredited with dying well and may well have succumbed to consumption.

LYDFORD (ST PETROC)

At Lydford not far from Tavistock is 'The Watchmaker's Tomb'. The engraved slab which once formed the top of a table tomb close to the porch is now preserved from the elements by being affixed to the interior north wall of the church. It runs:

Here lies in horizontal position
The outside case of
George Routleigh, Watchmaker
Whose abilities in that line were an honour
To his profession
Integrity was his mainspring,
And prudence the regulator
Of all the actions of his life.

Humane, generous and liberal
His hand never stopped
Till he had relieved distress.
So nicely regulated were all his motions
That he never went wrong
Except when set agoing
By people
Who did not know
His key
Even then he was easily
Set right again.
He had the art of disposing his time
So well
That his hours glided away
In one continual round
Of pleasure and delight
Till an unlucky minute put a period to
His existence.
He departed this life
Nov. 14 1802
Aged 57
Wound up
In hopes of being taken in hand
By his Maker
And of being thoroughly cleaned, repaired
And set agoing
In the world to come.

This epitaph appears to be totally unique, probably because the departed would need to be a watchmaker in order to use it? The earliest example of the text appearing in print seems to date from an American publication circa 1925. (D. McKay, Phipadelphia) so it was not widely disseminated during the nineteenth century.

UGBOROUGH (ST PETER)

A memorial which speaks for itself may be found in the north transept and commemorates 'TWO AFFECTIONATE BROTHERS' Mr Thomas

King (50) who died on 13th January 1792 and Mr John King (55) who passed away on 26th January 1795.

How Great must their Advantage be
How much their Pleasure Prove
Where Brethren dwell together
In Unity and Love.

ARLINGTON (ST JAMES)

Another epitaph which speaks for itself is that of Mr John Meadows who was an architect. His memorial in the church states that his place of residence was the parish of St John's Westminster, although this may well be simply a case of a town or business address. He died on 26th September 1791 aged 59 years.

Nature had stamp'd upon his mien a smile
That mark'd his mind insensible of guile
And industry that marks the better Man,
He gain'd respect byond what titles can.

SIDMOUTH (ST GILES AND ST NICHOLAS)

A mural tablet in the south aisle dedicated to Mary wife of Robert Lisle who died 21st February 1791 aged 39, who

'By her own desire lies buried here'.

BLEST WITH SOFT AIRS FROM HEALTH-RESTORING SKIES,
SIDMOUTH, TO THEE THE DROOPING PATIENT FLIES,
AH! NOT UNFAILING IS THY PORT TO SAVE ,
TO **HER** *THOU GAVEST NO REFUGE BUT A GRAVE:*
GUARD IT MILD SIDMOUTH AND REVERSE ITS STORE,
MORE PRECIOUS NONE SHALL EVER TOUCH THY SHORE.

The tablet states that Mary came from Acton House, Northumberland. On the evidence of the epitaph she came south for reasons of health. One wonders why Mary asked to be buried in Sidmouth. Perhaps she was unhappy in the North? Her husband Robert acknowledged one natural son in his will dated 1799 and had remarried producing more children before his own demise.

LAMERTON (ST PETER)

In this case I am putting the details of exactly who the grave holds first in order to clarify the epitaph fully.

Here lieth the sleeping dust of Renald Strout of this Parish Yeom. He was buried the 22nd day of July in the 50th year of his Age 1787. Also John son of Renald and Mary Strout was here buried the 19th day of decr 1766 Aged three years.

Reader behold here in the dust we lie
Convincing proof that youth and age must die
A tender son with his indulgent father
Here in this silent grave shall rest together
Untill that awful day the Angell swore
Before his God that time shall be no more
Than we shall quit this tenement of day
And Joyn the saints in realms of endless day
Trust not in youth all flesh is like the grass
The flowers fade away their beautys pass
So short my life so soon by death cut down
And earth exchanged for an immortal Crown.

There is here a use of capitals somewhat at odds with modern practice. There is little doubt that many of the abbreviations used at the top of the inscription ‘Here lieth…’ were to enable this rather lengthy piece to be accommodated on a reasonably sized stone.

STOKE GABRIEL (ST GABRIEL)

In memory of Elizabeth, daughter of Walter Drew, wife of Henry Dugdall who departed this life March 19th, 1762 in the 32nd year of her age.

Reader thou may’st forbear to weep

For her who in this Grave does sleep
Such Charitable drops would best be giveen
To those who late or never came to Heaven
But here you would by weeping on this Dust
Allay her Happiness with thy mistrust
Whose pious closing of her Youthful Years
Deserves thy imitation not thy tears

Underneath the poem it states that she rests 'near this place'.

BICKINGTON (ST MARY THE VIRGIN)

I from my Earthly friends am sent
And to my Heavenly Father bent
Dear Friends for me lament no more
I am not lost but gone before.

This inscription appears on a ledger stone in the north aisle of the church marking the grave of Mary Bickford who died 30th October 1736 aged 30. The stone is in poor condition thus it is not possible to say if the poem was inscribed in 1736 or when Mary's husband followed her to the grave in 1765 (aged 55). However the wording suggests the earlier date. I would conject that the stone was broken when it was prised upwards with a crow-bar to allow the addition of a second coffin to what I imagine is a small brick-lined vault beneath? The surface is also rather worn by many generations of worshippers' feet.

MORETONHAMPSTEAD (ST ANDREW)

In the porch Francis Waldren who died 2nd October 1731 has this brief epitaph:

Angels on Earthly Visits make but little stay:
And Heavenly Minds to Heaven soon find their way.

TAWSTOCK (ST PETER)

Robert Lovett Esq '...dyed of Malignant Small Pox ye 27th November 1710...' This endemic killer was no respecter of class; on his memorial plaque it runs:

Mount Pious Soul up on the wings of Love,
To the Bright Mansions of the Blest above,
Leave here they Dust, to Loftier things Aspire
Go bear a part in the Celestial Quoir:
Whilst here on Earth, it was thy chiefest care,
To serve thy Maker in his house of prayer,
Zeal for Religion did thy heart command
Pity thine Eye and Charity thine Hand,
So Calm a death after such well spent years
Calls for our Imitation, not our Tears.

STOKE GABRIEL (ST GABRIEL)

Memorial plaque in the chancel in memory of Tamosin the wife of Peter Lyde. She died 23rd February 1663. Like many early memorials this one does not record her age.

LONG MAY THY NAME AS LONG AS MARBLE LAST
BELOVED TAMOSIN THOUGH UNDER CLODS HER CAST
THIS FORMALL HEART DOTH TRULY SIGNIFY
TWIXT WIFE AND HUSBAND CORDIELL UNITY
IF TO BE GRACCIUS DOTH REQUIR DUE PRAISE
LET TAMOSIN HAVE IT SHE DESERVS YE BAYES

I have not been able to determine the precise meaning of *YE BAYES*.

BARNSTAPLE (ST PETER)

A typical seventeenth-century wall plaque commemorates Mrs Amy Tooker the wife of Mr John Tooker. She died on 7th December 1656.

Tis not Her Plenteous issue nor this Pile,

Her Husband's Love erected, can beguile.
Times stroying hand, for such Memorials must
Themselves ly downe wrapt in Oblivions Dust
No shee Preferu'd Her Name.
A way more Sure.
By Faith, Love, Patince A meek Life and Pure.
There these are Spices shall Enbawime Her Name,
And make it Fragrant, when the Worlds A Flame.

N.B. This plaque may have been restored during the twentieth century just possibly adding confusion regarding the first two words of the penultimate line. In the third line *'stroying'* is the modern *destroying*. *Enbawime* = embalm.

EXETER (ST MARTIN)

A plaque dedicated to Mrs Elizabeth Butler (grandchild of Thomas Spicer an Exeter alderman).

She died 27th October 1644.

SO GOOD A NEIGHBOUR MOTHER FRIEND AND WIFE
THAT HEAVEN & EARTH ABOVE HER WERE AT STRIFE
EARTH WAS DESIROUS HERE TO HAVE HER REST
HEAVEN WAS DESIROUS THERE TO HAVE HER BLEST
TO PLEASE THEM BOTH. HERSELF IN TWAIN DIVIDES
EARTH HAS THE BODYE. THE SOUL IN HEAVEN RESIDES

EXETER ST MARTIN

A further plaque in this church which is cared for by the Churches Conservation Trust is dedicated to Mrs Ivdeath (i.e. Judith) Wakeman widow, the daughter of Thomas Spicer (alderman). She died 5th January 1643.

THIS IS MY DWELLING
THIS IS MY TREWEST HOME
A HOUSE OF CLAY BEST FITTS A GUEST OF LOME
NAY TIS MY HOWSE FOR I PCEAVE I HAVE

IN ALL MY LIFE BYN WALKING TO THIS GRAVE. (SIC)

N.B. PCEAVE = perceive, BYN = been.

NEWTON ST CYRES (ST CYR AND ST JULITTA)

This epitaph seems to be something of a riddle. Certainly one needs to take some time to think about what the poet is trying to say! I have departed from my usual practice with the transcription of this poem; since it was written at a time when the letters which we read as I and V also stood for J and U. To make it easier to read I have stuck to the modern usage; however I have not altered the actual spelling in any other way. The reader will of course note however that *OR* is the modern OUR and that *DOME* is an older spelling of doom.

This monument is dedicated to Sir John Northcote who died in December 1632 and was erected by his son (also John) in the year 1637. Sir John and both of his wives are commemorated here but the epitaph that I have chosen is that of his second wife Susannah who bore him a great many children.

JEHOVAH FIRST COMPOSED US TWO IN ONE
THEN MADE ONE TWO, TIL STRONG AFFECTION DID REUNITE
US ONE, DEATH TRIED HIS SKILL
TO PART US AGAINE, BUT COULD NOT WORKE HIS WILL
ONE WAS OUR HOPE, FAITH, COMFORT, ONE'S OR TOMBE
ONE PLACE OUR SOULE HATH, TIL THE DAY OF DOME.

Rightly I think included here also is the epitaph of what must surely be Susannah Northcote's daughter Anna. The monument tells us that she was Sir John's daughter who had married John Elford, but does not specify by which wife; but the reference to 'Old ANNA' gives the clue that Susannah was her mother who 'creept to Christ' e.g. lived a long time' The plaque is not dated nor does it give any age but probably dates from the 1640s:

Short was her life, that long may heer lye dead.
Who dy'd to live and raigne w'th Christ her head.
Old ANNA creept to Christ, young ANNA flyes

Into his bosome: for to wedd him dyes,
If grace of virtue, could have life retayn'd,
She 'ad beene immortal: and heer still remayn'd

Then heaven should want one to sing in her quire,
The saints sweet Antheame Wch let's all desire,
Where'ere shee came true love of all shee gott,
Depraving Enuye could her fame ne'r blott
Her mate that left her, found her of that prise,
As shee gain'd the heavens, he lost ear ths paradise,
Yet mourne not too much,
For shee does but sleep,
To wake and meet thee,
Wher eyes ne'r shall weep.

N.B. Antheame = modern anthem; Enuye = modern any.

BRANSCOMBE (ST WINIFRED)

Anne Bartlett the widow of Ellys Bartlett Gent. Died at the age of 47 on 31st January 1606. Her monument appears to have been erected in 1608 judging by the date 20th December 1608 which is written at the very top next to this verse:

WHEN DEATH DID ME ASSAYLE
TO GOD THEN DID I CRYE
OF JACOBES WELL TO MOYSTE MY SOULE
THAT IT MIGHT NEVER DYE

This appears to be a (biblical) reference to St John's Gospel chapter 4 verses 1-42. This was a well from which Jesus once drunk and in the passage Christ states '*...whoever drinks of the water that I shall give him shall never thirst; the water which I shall give him will become in him a spring of water welling up to eternal life.*'

Mary Martin's headstone (Tavistock St Eustachius). A reminder that we will all *be eaten by worms was not uncommon in Georgian and Victorian England.*

This colourful seventeenth-century epitaph has been restored to its former glory by The Churches Conservation Trust under whose care this redundant church now is. (Exeter St Martin).

Joseph Bray's headstone is broken in two; the top portion is propped against the north wall of the churchyard. (Walkhampton).

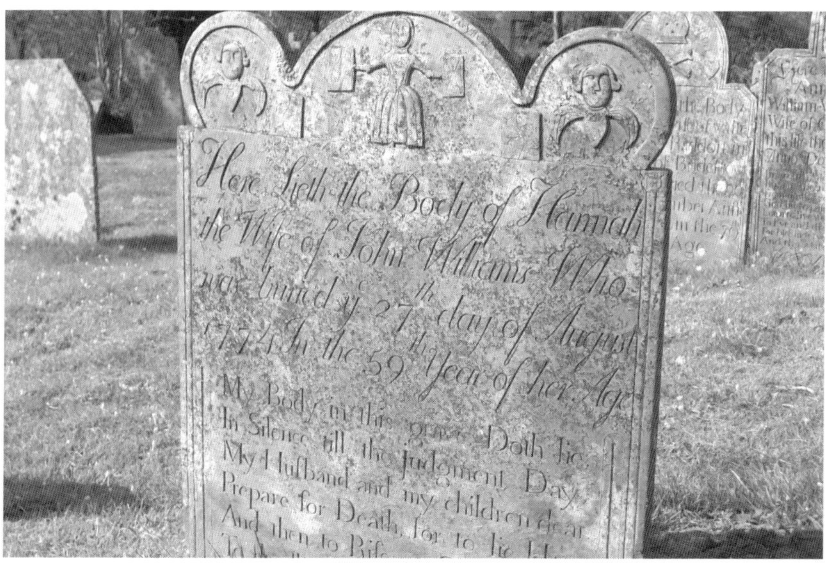

The slate headstone of Hannah Williams – the theme of this epitaph was commonplace during the eighteenth century. (Lydford St Petroc).

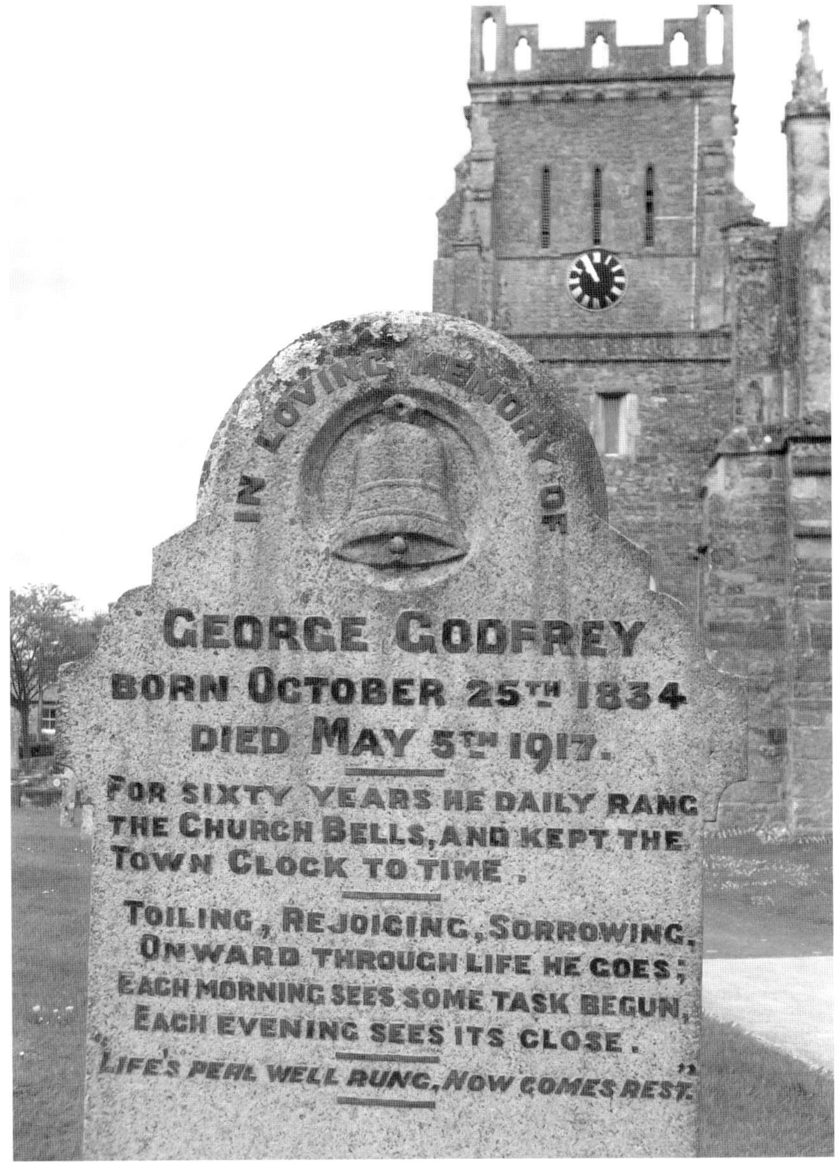

George Godfrey's headstone with an extract from a Longfellow poem. (Ottery St Mary).

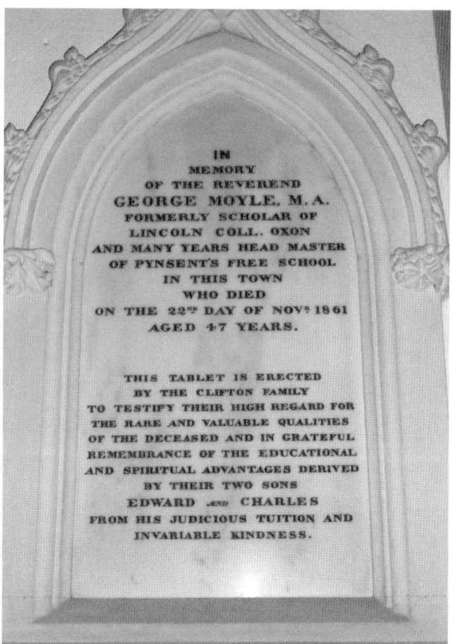

The informative headstone of an old soldier. (Gittisham).
Right: *Memorial to a local headmaster. (Chudleigh).*

In Georgian England a relief *of an urn often surmounted memorial plaques but by the mid-Victorian period a scene depicting grief (albeit with acceptance of death being God's will) is sometimes found. (Chudleigh).*

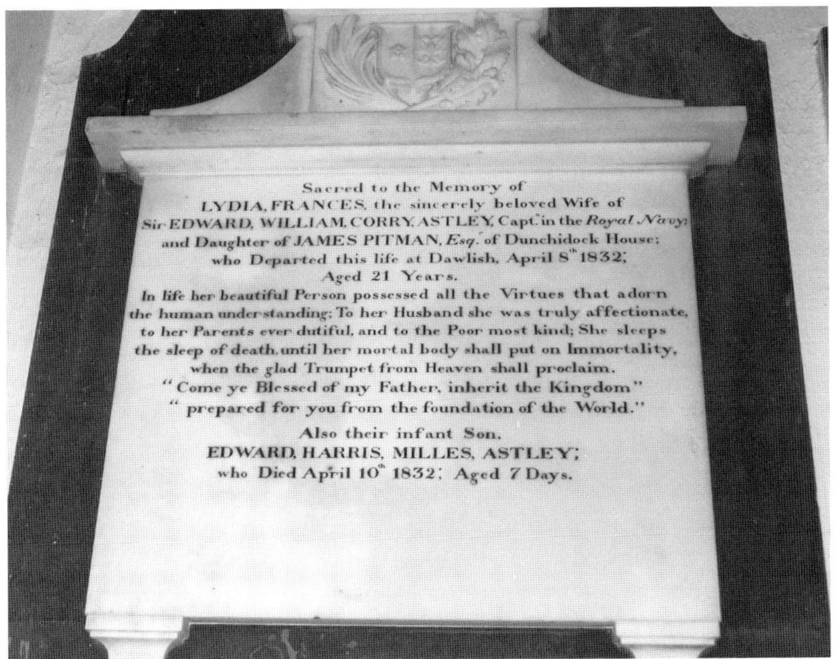

Sacred to the Memory of
LYDIA, FRANCES, the sincerely beloved Wife of
Sir EDWARD, WILLIAM, CORRY, ASTLEY, Capt. in the Royal Navy;
and Daughter of JAMES PITMAN, Esq. of Dunchidock House;
who Departed this life at Dawlish, April 8th 1832;
Aged 21 Years.
In life her beautiful Person possessed all the Virtues that adorn
the human understanding; To her Husband she was truly affectionate,
to her Parents ever dutiful, and to the Poor most kind; She sleeps
the sleep of death, until her mortal body shall put on Immortality,
when the glad Trumpet from Heaven shall proclaim.
"Come ye Blessed of my Father, inherit the Kingdom"
"prepared for you from the foundation of the World."
Also their infant Son,
EDWARD, HARRIS, MILLES, ASTLEY;
who Died April 10th 1832; Aged 7 Days.

There are a number of memorials to the Pitman family in Dunchideock church. Lydia, who had married Sir Edward Astley must like so many young women have died as a result of childbirth; her son who lived but a few days is commemorated with her.

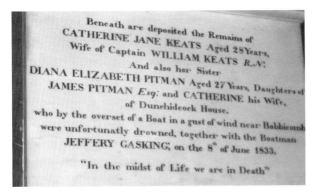

Beneath are deposited the Remains of
CATHERINE JANE KEATS Aged 28 Years,
Wife of Captain WILLIAM KEATS R.N.
And also her Sister
DIANA ELIZABETH PITMAN Aged 27 Years, Daughters of
JAMES PITMAN Esq. and CATHERINE his Wife,
of Dunchideock House,
who by the overset of a Boat in a gust of wind near Babbicomb
were unfortunatly drowned, together with the Boatman
JEFFERY GASKING, on the 8th of June 1833.
"In the midst of Life we are in Death"

Not strictly speaking an epitaph but in the days before death certificates a useful source of information for family historians. (Dunchideock).

Henry Fothergill is buried in the chancel of Cheriton Bishop church. His epitaph is on the north wall of the chancel.

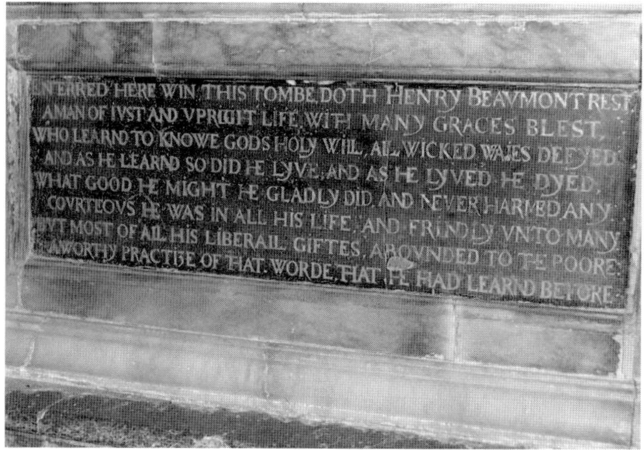

Above and right: *The tomb of Henry Beaumont (d. 1st April 1591) who built nearby Combe House. (Gittisham).*

Henry Beaumont (left) kneels in prayer above his epitaph, as his wife (right) kneels behind him south aisle of Gittisham church.

Detail of a seventeenth-century monument. (Newton St Cyres).

A verse from a hymn is used as Jane Moore's epitaph. (Pancrasweek).

An epitaph for worn-out bell clappers. (Coryton).

Bridestowe churchyard has an unusual number of table-tombs.

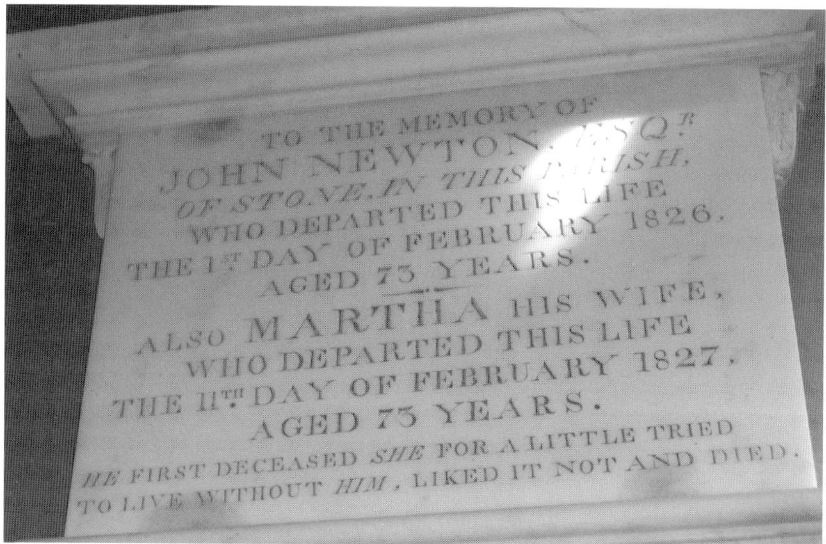

This plaque speaks for itself. (Bridestowe).

Detail from the memorial to Eliza Mortimer who died 6th June 1826 aged 16. (Exeter St Martin).

EPITAPHS FOR THE OVER SIXTIES

OTTERY ST MARY (ST MARY)

In the southern part of the churchyard not far from the south wall of the chancel and in sight of the south tower lies the grave of George Godrey who died on 5th May 1917 aged 82.

FOR SIXTY YEARS HE DAILY RUNG THE CHURCH BELLS,
AND KEPT THE TOWN CLOCK TO TIME.

'TOILING, REJOICING,SORROWING,
ONWARD THROUGH LIFE HE GOES;
EACH MORNING SEES SOME NEW TASK BEGUN,
EACH EVENING SEES ITS CLOSE'

'LIFES' PEAL WELL RUNG,
NOW COMES REST'

The poem here is a truncated verse from *The Village Blacksmith* by Longfellow.

BUSTFASTLEIGH (HOLY TRINITY)

'LIFES WORK WELL DONE, NOW COMES REST'

On the gravestone of Clare the wife of James Chaffe who died 26th April 1898 aged 53 and James Chaffe who died on 28th April 1915 aged 68.

This short verse clearly a variant of that found at Ottery St Mary is apparently still in vogue being suggested for use by www.cemeterymemorials.net a U.K. company based in the east of England.

EXETER (ST DAVID)

On the gravestone of John Callaway Guest born 1821 who died 5th May 1901 is an appropriate epitaph for the former voluntary organist of The Mint Methodist Church in Exeter:

When we appear in yonder cloud
With all the ransomed throng
Then will we sing, more sweet, more loud
And Christ shall be our song.

N.B. Where specific other denominational burial grounds or public cemeteries did not exist Methodists and other non-conformist denominations, also Roman Catholics, were often buried in Church of England churchyards.

BUCKFASTLEIGH (HOLY TRINITY)

A light is from our household gone
The voice we loved is still'd
A place is vacant in our home
Which never can be fill'd

Found on the gravestone of Ann Gilpin who died 17th January 1894 aged 67 years.

BRIDESTOWE (ST BRIDGET)

Weep not! The land to which I go is beautiful and bright;
There shall tears of sorrow flow,
And there shall be no night.
Rejoice! We yet shall meet again,
Where none may say farewell,
And in our home of deathless love,
Together we shall dwell.

Headstone of David Yelland died 26th January 1870 aged 62.

PANCRASWEEK (ST PANCRAS)

Our flesh shall slumber in the ground,
Till the last trumpet's joyful sound:
Then burst the chains with sweet surprise,
And in our SAVIOUR'S image rise.

Grave of Richard Fanson who died 24th March 1865 aged 81 years. He outlived his wife Catherine (69) and daughter Ann (28) both of whom died in1854.

N.B. This verse can also be found in at least two different hymn books published in the United States. It was published as verse 4 of Hymn No. 816 in *The Sabbath Hymn Book for the service of Song in the House of the Lord.* New York (Mason Brothers-Broadway) 1858. Source http://books.google.com. It is also found in a devotional work by the minister of the Presbyterian Church at Salem N.Y. entitled *The Ruin and Recovery of Man…* Pub. J.P. Reynolds, Salem N.Y. (1813). The earliest usage that I have noted is at Rockingham, Vermont, on the grave of Betty Lane aged 33 who died 22nd June 1791 and her two un-named infants. (Source www.kwkautz.com). Another early example in England is at the Baptist Burial ground in Nottingham for Sarah Cullen aged 48 and four infant children in 1797. (Source www.genuki.org.uk).

PANCRASWEEK (ST PANCRAS)

Of William Beckley who died on the 27th day of March 1854, aged 60 years, it is recorded that:

> He was a man of sound piety, mature judgement and of unblemished character: had been a *Member* of the *Methodist Society* upwards of forty years:
> And nearly the whole of that time a useful *Class leader* and an acceptable *Local Preacher*.
> He died respected and respected and regretted by all classes;
> But death, though sudden found him ready to enter into the joy of his LORD.

A further example of a non-conformist being buried in a Church of England churchyard.

HOLSWORTHY (ST PETER AND ST PAUL))

Octogenarian Elizabeth Meyrick was a maiden lady and the eldest daughter of the late rector who received the glowing accolades often given to clergy and their families.

In addition to the text 'Blessed are the dead which die in the Lord' (from Revelations 14:13) we find:

> *She bore her long and severe illness, with Christian patience, resigning herself to his will, and reposing in faith and hope on the merits of our blest redeemer.*
>
> *As a daughter and sister she was truly affectionate; as a friend ever ready with sound and kind counsel; as a benefactress to the poor ever happy to relieve them. Until it pleased God to call her hence from time unto eternity.*

Mural tablet on the wall of the south aisle in the church commemorating Elizabeth Meyrick who died 28th June 1853 aged 83 years.

EXMOUTH (POINT IN VIEW CHAPEL – FORMERLY CONGREGATIONAL; NOW AFFILIATED TO THE UNITED REFORM CHURCH) NEAR A' LA RONDE

The eccentric and well travelled Parminter cousins are well-known for the building of their *round* house *A' La Ronde* now owned by the National Trust on the outskirts of Exmouth. The cousins are commemorated on a plaque in the nearby chapel known as *Point in View* (and formerly of the Congregationalist denomination) which they also caused to be built for their own use when they found it too hard to travel in to Exmouth itself. Jane died 6th November 1811 although her cousin Mary did not follow until 18th December 1849. Whilst these verses are perhaps not unique, I include them as their subjects are so well known. It seems to me that these lines would be more appropriate to husband and wife; I imagine that they were chosen as these two spinster ladies were in life very close.

Here sleep! No noise shall break thy rest,
Till the Last Trump proclaim thee wholly blest;
Then shall thy former partner claim each dust,
And both in one made perfect join the just.

LYDFORD (ST PETROC)

From years of sorrow and of pain, The Lord hath set me free: Your loss is my eternal gain, Prepare to follow me.

Probably constructed from a series of short quotations or ideas joined together this is an entirely typical example of the run of the mill Victorian epitaph. It is found on the headstone of Elizabeth Gill aged 80 died 29th June 1841. Her son John Gill did not follow until 1875 and is commemorated on the same stone aged 84.

CORYTON (ST ANDREW)

Here, mortal man, behold thy doom,
And now learn wisdom from the tomb;
Darkness and silence here impart,
A lesson which should reach thy heart;
That in the dust thou soon must rest,
And none but saints with Christ are blest.

Grave of Henry Symons died 29th May 1840, aged 66.

WALKHAMPTON (ST MARY THE VIRGIN)

So as I now am gone before
Besure erelong you must ,
When you have run'd out natures race
Be turned into dust.

Grave of Abraham Giles who died 16th June 1838 aged 66 years.

BRIDESTOWE (ST BRIDGET)

Thrice happy they, who safely wafted o'er, Death's rapid stream, experience grief no more;
From suff'rings free, they sing in sweetest lays, The Saviour's triumph and exalt his praise,
Reader, whoe'er thou art, at once be wise; Renounce the world. And seek the Heavenly prize, 'Tis Christ that calls, his gracious voice obey; time flies – death hastens – why should you delay?

Grave of Thomas Medland who died 14th February 1826 aged 74 and his wife Mary who died only a week later.

PAIGNTON (ST JOHN THE BAPTIST)

In the churchyard the grave of John Moore died 31st October 1821 aged 71 years.

Industrious, Frugal and what not,
Upright and Honest, tho' but poor;
What ever Titles Valour got
Virtue and Love had MOORE.

Next to this stone lay what I speculate are John's wife's remains; she predeceased him on 18th December 1810. Although her age is not recorded one might assume that she was somewhat younger. Her epitaph runs:

My Loving Husband, I bid Adieu
I leave my Children to God & you
My Children Dear, love each other
And Comfort your affected Father

WALKHAMPTON (ST MARY THE VIRGIN)

While here on earth a true and faithful friend
Esteeme'd by those who knew him to the end:
But summond hence,

He moulders here in dust
Till Christ shall say Arise come forth ye just.

Grave of Richard Adams who died 9th November 1801 aged 93 years.

Also of Mary his wife who died 5th January 1822 aged 78 years.

EXETER (ST MARTIN)

On the south wall of this redundant church (although formerly in the now demolished church of St Paul Exeter) is John Codington's memorial.

This memorial is included as another example of the often seen theme of the expectation of a successful and happy life snatched away by a premature end. Let the monument however tell its own sad but not unusual tale.

Sacred to the memory of John Codington Esqr. *Of this city…*

N.B. John died in 1801 at the age of 70 and his wife Mary predeceased him in 1795 at the age of 60; however they were good ages and would have been no cause of remark.

…And of SAMUEL and SARAH, their son and daughter, who died in the bloom of youth, while hope illumined every scene, and embellished future prospects with delusive expectations of prosperity and happiness.

MARIA

Wife of BARTOHOLOMEW PARR of this city M.D. the only remaining child and sister, had with deep regret directed this monument to be raised as a testimony of her affection of her affection and grief, but before its completion was herself consigned to the same tomb at the early age of XXXIII years. An. MDCCCIII.

GREAT TORRINGTON (ST MICHAEL)

Now virtually obscured by the organ casing in the north aisle of this large church and probably not having been in public view for above one hundred years:

Replete with all the forms of labour'd Praise,
The sculptur'd Monument let others raise,
Dear Parents tho' deep Sorrow graves the line,
Your numerous Virtues will not mark this Shrine,
The Mind that best can witness best will know,
Their proper Eulogy is not below,
From these abodes translated to the Skies,
Before your God the full Memorial lies.

This wall plaque was placed by the children of John Palmer (Gentleman) who died 14th September 1770 aged 61 and also commemorates his wife Mary who outlived him by almost 24 years and who died on 27th May 1794 aged 78. Clearly the monument was erected after the mother's death and would have occupied a prominent position until the organ was installed, probably in the 1860s.

Sadly (and certainly disappointingly for the relatives who placed such memorials in the belief that their words would be visible to all in perpetuity) the installation of organs (as hymn singing became part of the Anglican services in the mid-Victorian period) often obscured the memorials of earlier generations. This was and remains a universal problem.

CORYTON (ST ANDREW)

You Readers all prey cast your Eye
Upon these lines as you pass by
And think how soon the time may be
You may lie in the dust like me
Repent with speed make no delay
That Christ may wash your sins away.

Grave of William Combe died 22nd July 1785 aged 82.

N.B. The theme, repentance in order to be prepared, in case death should also take the passer by without warning is a common one which was to remain popular throughout the following century.

SOURTON (ST THOMAS A' BECKET)

Joseph Pleace a yeoman farmer was buried just to the west of the tower on 13th November 1783. On his headstone it reads:

Numbere'd among thy people I
Desire with joy thy face to see
Jesus thou didst for sinners die
Thy Death hath purchase'd Life for me.

TIVERTON (ST PETER)

Samuel Newte had been the rector of nearby Tidecombe. He died on 18th February 1781 at the age of 65. His 'surviving sons' erected this monument in the church.

I

The Bitterness of Death is pass'd – and now*
Loos'd from the tortur'd Frame of human Earth
Fly, PARENT SPIRIT, to the Source of Peace!
Where first th' immortal Soul receiv'd it's Birth.

II

There stands the Saviour, and the Friend of Man.
And now he calls thee from a World of Woe;
Come, faithful Servant, take the Christian Crown,
*"Tis won by Virtue in the Storms below"***

III

Far hence be flattery – but impartial Truth
Her honest Judgement shall to Time consign.

Let Emulation read without a Sigh,
Nee'r spake Religion from a Voice like thine.

IV

Now if the exalted Dead can ask a Gift
From Heavn's all-ruling Lord, Oh! FATHER HEAR
Ask it for those, whom Duty bids to raise
This weak Memorial to a Name so dear.

V

Yet not for mortal Gifts their Prayer ascends,
Be this their Wish, while Nature pours its Breath.
Oh! May they bear the Toils of Life like thee,
And meet thee at the Throne of Heav'n, in Death.

*pass'd i.e. modern usage = 'past'. ** 'Tis won…' seems to be a brief quotation from Dante's *Divine Comedy*.

LYDFORD (ST PETROC)

On either side of the stone *Time how short* and *Eternity how long*. After the details of the departed, John Friend buried 16th Oct. 1780, comes the inscription:

Behold this stone, I here entombed must lie. Convincing proof, that you and all shall die. But Oh, from earth to heaven we take our flight. To see the saints in Glory with delight. The joys that angels prize and men adore. There we again shall meet, to part no more.

SOURTON (ST THOMAS A' BECKET)

When five & thirty years Expire'd then I
Resine my breath & being born to die
Leaving this vitall world in hopes to rise
To meet my Lord in Everlasting joys

To hear ye joyfull Sentence come ye blest
And Enter in to Everlasting rest.

Beneath this inscription is also written:

Remember friends what I have spoken
Let never more my grave be broken.

One occasionally meets the reminder that a grave should never be interfered with. During the twentieth century a number of churchyards were cleared of headstones in order to make grass cutting easier and thus cheaper. In these cases, even where a plan of the graves exists, it can be well near impossible to find the actual resting place of the departed. Luckily Sourton has taken heed of these words.

Agnes Pleace was in fact 34 years old at the time of her death and was buried in the churchyard on 14th May 1749. She was the daughter of William and Agnes Pleace, yeoman farmers.

CHITTLEHAMPTON (ST HIERITHA)

Possibly as a deliberate counter to the verbose excesses and hyperbole of some contemporary epitaphs the memorial to Samuel Rolle aged 66 who died in 1734, his wife (d. 1735) and their son Samuel (d. 1746) although a large memorial has but a few words inscribed upon it; after the list of the *departed* it runs:

Whose lives have left to Posterity
A more expressive memorial
Than can be perpetuated
On
The most durable Marble.

DUNTERTON (ALL SAINTS)

Matthew Wrayford who died on 16th June 1714 was the son of the former incumbent Thomas Wrayford (see next entry) and he also has an interesting epitaph; no age is given but it seems probable that he like his father exceeded the threescore and ten years.

For Soul, and Body,
'twas their Chiefest Care,
Some good Insytructions,
Cordials to Prepare.
'till GOD by Death, did
Warn them to Forbear.

DUNTERTON (ALL SAINTS)

Thomas Wrayford was the rector of Dunerton long before the Civil War. He survived Cromwell's Protectorate and was still the rector long after the Restoration of King Charles, dying on 9th November 1678. His epitaph is on a slate plaque in the small chancel. It runs:

Here lyes my dust, but I do live above,
Earths grave ye Raven hides, heaven's Ark ye dove
Sure both shall live; this body shall arise when
Doomesday Comes, Earth's Generall Assise.

Thomas' age is not recorded but as he became rector in 1630 it seems reasonable to suppose that he was in his mid-seventies. One source (www.flicker.com) suggests that he was born in 1601 and states that he was also rector of Warleggan (Cornwall) from 1660-1661.He was survived by his wife but only for a few weeks, as she died the February following.

CHITTLEHAMPTON (ST HIERITHA)

The Reverend John Bear M.A. described in this *Commonwealth Period* as *pastor* of this church died on 5th February 1656 aged 67. His epitaph in the church demands:

Stay reader: it will profit thee to know
Who 'tis that lies enshrined here below
A man whose worth & answerable paines
(more for the Churches Good, than his own gaines)
Did render him desir'd His care was still

To speak his Masters minde, & doe his will.
Thus (Factor-like) his studious heart did burn
To make home to his Lord some good return
Of souls for Heaven
And now, heark how hee sings triumphant
Praises to the King of Kings.

N.B. *Factor-like = presumably modern 'as a benefactor'.*

MORETONHAMPSTED (ST ANDREW)

Francis Whiddon M.A. had been the minister of this small moorland town for 32 years when he died on 5th January 1656. He had seen the parish through the reign of Charles I, the Civil War and much of Cromwell's 'reign'.

His epitaph is inside the church just above the doorway on the south wall. It runs:

Lo here the watchman fallen asleep
The Pastor that this flock did keep
This Jacobs labours now are done.
He's gone to take his rest thereon
Now planet meteor falling light
In's orb he shin'd a star most bright
Christs hand did hold him while he went
His circuit in this firmament
Weep Moreton think ont don't forget
Thy Cynosura now is sett
Yet he's but chang'd the faint not dies
This day star only sets to rise. (sic)

It must have taken some fortitude to see the local church through these troubled years which saw Archbishop Laud's efforts to return beauty to worship in the 1630s, then the Civil War followed by a period when in theory the Prayer Book was replaced with The Directory of Public Worship.

N.B. Cynosura was in Greek Mythology a nymph from Crete who at one time nursed Zeus when he was being hidden from Chronus. Her name is also sometimes given to the star Polaris.

BARNSTAPLE (ST PETER)

A rather large mural plaque commemorates Edward Ferris, a merchant and twice Mayor of this town. He died in 1649 aged 63. This epitaph is in two sections. The first runs:

READER, IF THOU WOULDS'T KNOW THE GEMME THAT LYES
CAS'D IN THIS MARBLE, FIRST ASKE THE POORES EYES
WHO THAT THEY MAY PRESERVE THEIR DEAR LOSSE SAFE
WRITE IN THEIR LASTING TEARES HIS EPITAPH
THEN READ THE SCHOOLE BY HIM ENDOW'D T'ADVANCE ARTS
'BOVE OUR MONSTER – TEEMING IGNORANCE
IF NEXT, YOULD LEARNE THE PRUDENCE OF THE GOWNE
AND HOW HE HELD THE SCALES
ASKE THE WHOLE TOWNE
BUT LASTLY, VIEW THIS PLACE WHICH THOUGH IT IS GODS
HOUSE BY RIGHT HIS ZEAL YET MADE IT HIS
HERE HE WOULD DWELL
HERE HE FULL OFT HATH BEEN TO SPEAKE TO GOD AND HEAR
GOD SPEAKE TO HIM

Below is inscribed:

So that to write his Epitaph must be
To picture Justice Arts Faith Charity
Let marble quarrys then els where be spent
Not stones but deeds build up his monument
Reader this tombe speaks not unto thy eyes
But to thy hands Go thou and do likewise.

N.B. Like the majority of earlier epitaphs, the ravages of time and the archaic use (or rather lack) of punctuation gives rise to minor confusion. In the case of this plaque I have chosen to leave out all of the surviving punctuation since it is not clear which are commas and full stops and which are in fact imperfections or blotches.

ARLINGTON (ST JAMES)

An unusual and rather large ledger stone can be found on the south inside wall of the tower, which is the only part of the structure to survive from the original edifice. Presumably the stone was originally set in the floor of the church prior to a rebuild which was undertaken in 1846. It may have marked the vault which contains the mortal remains of one David Harris who died 16th September 1648 aged 73, and his wife Alice who seems to have been considerably older. According to the inscription which is very clear, she died 2nd June 1640 aged 82.

'FRIEND STAY OBSERVE THIS TRUTHS FULLFILLED PLAINE'

'WHOME GOD CONJOIYNS FOR MAN TO PART'S VAINE
IN DEATH AS LIFE LOE STILL THEYRE LODGED NEER
BY DAVIDS SIDE HERE SLEEPS HIS ALICE DEER
HER FAITH AND HOPE IN CHRIST THE SAME LIKE HIS
THE SAMES HER SHARE IN HEAVNS ETERNAL BLISS'

N.B. It was necessary to change a few characters to the modern usage to make this epitaph clearer.

CORYTON (ST ANDREW)

Three worn-out clappers from the bells in the tower were affixed to a board on the tower wall with the following epitaph:

Our duty done
In belfry high,
Now voiceless tongues
At rest we lie.

I was *absolutely* convinced that this epitaph and its usage were totally unique and was really surprised when I researched the lines in the later stages of editing this work to find them also in use for the exact same purpose in two churches in the east of England, one in Lincolnshire (St Nicholas, Addlethorpe) and the other in Suffolk (St Andrew's, Brockley). As a former bell-ringer I began to feel embarrassed by my own ignorance – no doubt some reader will one day provide me with the identity of the author? sources www.skegnessvideo.com,www.suffolkchurches.co.uk/brockley

To complete this anthology I include a short modern epitaph (2008) which I recently saw in a churchyard in North Devon.

'LIVE RESPECTED DIE REMEMBERED'

SOURCES BIBLIOGRAPHY

Books used or referred to in the text

Booker, Luke, (the Rev.), *Tributes to the Dead*, J.Hatchard & Son, London (1830)

Caldwell, Thomas, *A Collection of Epitaphs*, Lackington, Allen & Co., London (1802)

Hare, Augustus, *Epitaphs for Country Churchyards*, John Henry & James Parker, Oxford (1851)

Mogridge, G., *The Churchyard Lyrist*, Houlston & Wright, London (1832). Reprinted 1860

Parker, John, *Reading Latin Epitaphs*, Cressar Publications, Penzance (Fourth Edition 2004)

Tissington, Silvester, *A Collection of Epitaphs*, Simpkin, Marshal & Co., London (1857)

Other Sources

N.B. For the most part sources are referred to in the text.
Some statistics were obtained from www.gos.gov.uk and www.british-history.ac.uk

The typescript of Upton Pyne parish register is to be found in the Devon County Record Office at Exeter as is original of the letter describing the last days of the child Thomas Quicke (Newton St Cyres).

The reference to our lifespan being 'threescore years and ten' is taken from Psalm 90 verse 10. It runs *'The days of our age are threescore years and ten; and though men be so strong as that they come to fourscore years: yet is their strength then but labour and sorrow; so soon it passeth away, and we are gone'* I quote from the Book of Common Prayer version since until the revision of the lectionary in the twentieth century this was sung in church as one of the proper psalms for morning service on the 18th day of the month and would have been widely known.